WINDOWS FOR THE SOUL

Revised & Updated

Wardell
PUBLICATIONS INC

WINDOWS FOR THE SOUL

Revised and Updated

Ecclesiastic Art Glass at Bovard Studio

Ron Bovard

www.windowsforthesoul.com

Wardell

PUBLICATIONS INC

The Creative Work

THE CREATIVE WORK PRESENTED in this book is the result of the skill and craftsmanship of the entire team here at Bovard Studio both past and present. I especially would like to acknowledge the contribution of our lead designer, Sándor Fehér. I also would like to express my gratitude and appreciation to my publisher and editor Randy Wardell, whose sharp pen and keen eye added many improvements to this book.

Bovard Studio's fabulous glass painters and designers are an inspiration to watch. Through spending time with our artists I have gained a personal insight into how the studio system of artists, working in groups, resulted in the flowering of Renaissance art. I want to thank all our highly skilled craftspeople and our administrative staff who have devoted their life to this ancient tradition. They have created new stained glass art and have made a significant contribution to the preservation of our stained glass heritage through the repair and restoration of thousands of windows in religious sanctuaries, courthouses, state capitol buildings, libraries, hospitals, universities, and museums throughout the United States and abroad. Finally, everyone at Bovard Studio would like to express our gratitude and appreciation to our clients for the privilege of creating and preserving their stained glass heritage.

Ron Bovard

ACKNOWLEDGEMENTS

Photo of Ron Bovard on the project site of St. Mary of the Angels Church.

Contents

- Acknowledgements 4
- Introduction 7
1 The Mystery Of Ecclesiastic Art Glass 9
2 The Story Of Bovard Studio Inc. 12
3 A Mother's Love 17
4 Painted Medallions, Borders, & Rosettes 20
5 God's Test Of Faith 26
6 Salvaging History 28
7 Our Committee Has An Artist .30
8 West Angeles Cathedral Project .32
9 Creating Stained Glass Windows - An Overview 42
10 Design Development Process 44
11 Glass Selection And Fabrication 48
12 Butterfly Dreams Take Flight 57
13 Structure And Reinforcing 58
14 Protective Exterior Covering 60
15 Essential Elements For A Long Lasting Window 66
16 A Lot on Plum Street 68
17 An English Country Chapel 70
18 A Tapestry Of Inspirations 72
19 Category 4 Hurricane Iniki 74
20 Cleaning And Maintenance Of Leaded Windows 76
21 Faceted Glass (Dalle De Verre) Windows 79
22 St. Peter's Church In Ruins 82
23 A Bona Fide Artistic Challenge 84
24 A Small Brotherhood 88
25 Masonic Symbols in Glass 90
26 Eastern Visions of the Soul 92
27 A Tiffany Window Restoration 94
28 The Stained Glass Design Gallery 104
29 The Faceted Glass Gallery 140
30 The Rose Window Gallery 148
- Author's Show Journal 157
- Contact Information & Bibliography 158
- Index 159

AUTHOR
Ron Bovard

PROJECT MANAGER
Carole Wardell

LAYOUT & TYPOGRAPHY
Randy Wardell • Esteban Luna
Christine Arleij (Cover)
Sándor Fehér • Eleanor Jessup

EDITOR
Randy Wardell

PHOTOGRAPHY
Except as noted in the text, the photographs
were taken by Bovard Studio Inc. personnel.
Including: Ron Bovard • Paul Conley
Chris Dieter • Sándor Fehér • Rene Holmberg
Elizabeth Loescher • Joe McManis • Amy Stark

Cataloging in Publication Data

Bovard, Ron

Windows For The Soul: Ecclesiastic art glass at
Bovard Studio / Ron Bovard. - Revised and Updated

Includes Index

ISBN-13: 978-0-919985-50-6

ISBN-10: 0-919985-50-5

1. Bovard, Ron. 2. Glass painting and staining–USA.
3. Christian art and symbolism–United States.
4. Christian art and Symbolism–Modern period,
1500–United States. I.Title

NK5398.B68A4 2006 748.5'0973 C2005-907040-4

Printed in Thailand by Phongwarin Printing Ltd.
Published simultaneously in Canada and USA
E-mail: info@wardellpublications.com
Website: www.wardellpublications.com

A Desire To Share

THIS BOOK IS THE RESULT of an innate desire to share my art, my craft and some of my spiritual insights and impressions. I share my knowledge on the creation of art, execution of craft and the restoration of our stained glass heritage. I have included information on the design and fabrication of new stained glass windows and the maintenance and restoration of historic stained glass windows. In addition you will find an extensive portfolio presenting a cross section of Bovard Studio's stained glass projects.

On the deeper level, through the stories of our clients, I am able to share a few spiritual insights based on my personal experiences and perceptions.

To be human and by living a full life one gains more than knowledge, one gains a certain knowingness from within. I have been blessed with a vocation that allows me to explore and express that inner knowledge on a daily basis. This book is part of that expression.

Ron Bovard

Right: The center panel from a window titled 'Madonna and Christ Child' (see full window on page 120).

INTRODUCTION

PUBLICATIONS INC

To receive our electronic newsletter or to send suggestions please contact us by EMail at: info@wardellpublications.com or visit our web site at: www.wardellpublications.com

Christ in Gethsemane, window designed for the First Presbyterian Church in DeLand, Florida.

Jesus in the Temple, window designed for the First Presbyterian Church in DeLand, Florida.

The Good Shepherd, window designed for the First Presbyterian Church in DeLand, Florida.

Noah's Ark, window designed for the First Presbyterian Church in DeLand, Florida.

Divine Illumination

SUNDAY MORNING, a youth fidgets in the cold hard pew. He stares off into space as a flickering beam of deep mysterious light penetrates his consciousness. Thoughts of heaven and hell, mixed with flashes of divine illumination, filter through his mind. Momentarily his attention is drawn to the stained glass window of Christ praying in the garden at Gethsemane. The sunlight is transformed as it penetrates the stained glass to heighten the look of fresh innocence and eternal love on the face of Christ.

The young man's attention shifts to the window of Christ as a young boy standing in the temple before his inquisitors. The anguished expressions on the faces of the Rabbis suggest they are uncertain how to react. Trapped by convention they are left with no alternative except to issue a proclamation of "blasphemy" even as they stare into the eyes of God manifest in Christ.

The Good Shepherd window now petitions the boy in a whole new and different way. He begins to understand that all life is infinitely more valuable than the most precious of diamonds. Now with the assistance of sunlight filtered through the colored glass he is able to witness the manifestation of God's eternal love from within the Son of a common carpenter.

And over there near the back of the church, why hadn't he noticed the Noah's Ark window before? Again, as in time immemorial, the seed of faith is planted. Will the ground be fertile or barren? Hope springs eternal as the dove returns to the ark with a sprouted olive branch symbolizing that the love of God shines again on Earth.

For the boy sitting in the pew on this Sunday morning his thoughts are lost in these painted images of God's Son made manifest, and man. His experience is not about the art of stained glass rather it is about how the light passes through the glass to transform the images in his mind's eye. Ultimately the message will penetrate into the heart and soul of this inquisitive child.

Hope springs eternal as the love of God shines again on Earth. Concentrated drops of mankind's individual love trickle into the ocean of God's love, washing against the shores of time, manifest as pure potential waiting for the bather. - R.B.

Nativity window from Bovard Studio's standard full-figure series.

THE MYSTERY OF ECCLESIASTIC ART GLASS

Above: Detail of "The Temple Priests" from Tiffany Studios' Great Chapel window at Reid Memorial Presbyterian Church, Richmond, Indiana. Restored by Bovard Studio.

Above: Detail of "The Young Christ" from Tiffany Studios' Great Chapel window at Reid Memorial Presbyterian Church, Richmond, Indiana. Restored by Bovard Studio.

Left: Detail of "The Good Samaritan" window by Tiffany Studios at St. Luke's United Methodist Church, Dubuque, Iowa. Restored by Bovard Studio. See pages 94 - 103 for more windows from this church.

As if by mystical intervention he notices one last window. This time he sees the peaceful, loving face and gentle hand of "Christ Knocking at the Door". The choice of eternal life, is the choice of this young boy. Now with fresh eyes and an open heart he gazes unabashedly into the light of the ancient art of stained glass. For the first time in his young life he actually comprehends the spiritual link between his heart, mind and soul as the preacher continues on with Sunday service.

Above: Detail of "Temple Priests" from Tiffany Studio's great Chapel window at Reid Memorial Presbyterian Church, Richmond, Indiana. Restored by Bovard Studio.

Above: The peaceful, loving face and gentle hand of Christ Knocking at the Door. A reproduction in glass of the client's favorite painting. Created for the Berean Assembly of God Church, Des Moines, Iowa.

The love of God is a vast infinite ocean, ever present, omniscient, everywhere. An unhappy person is like a person in the dark, all one has to do is flip on the light switch and enjoy the light. The light switch is the power of our own attention, consciousness itself. - R.B.

THE STORY OF BOVARD STUDIO

Our Artists and Craftspeople

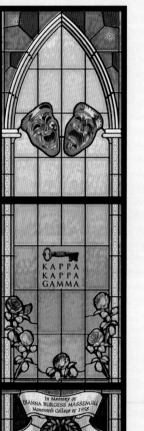

A memorial window designed for the theater auditorium, at Monmouth College, Monmouth, Illinois.

OVER THE PAST 20 YEARS Bovard Studio has grown from just myself to a staff of over 70 employees. Our artists and craftspeople embody some of the finest talent of our time. Our art department consists of eight glass painters and four designers originating from around the world. Our fabricators, restoration staff and installers have diverse backgrounds and skills as rich and varied as our artists. The majority of our staff are from the U.S.A. but we are truly fortunate to have artists from Argentina, Bulgaria, Canada, Germany, Hungary, Jamaica, Mexico and Ukraine.

Prior to establishing Bovard Studio I enjoyed a career as an independent artist for more than 20 years. During that time I was an active member of many artist guilds and trade organizations. Some of my most rewarding experiences occurred when my studio was located in a large warehouse space that accommodated many artists and their studios. The creative camaraderie and cooperative atmosphere was stimulating and I enjoyed working and studying in the company of those artists. However, due to the singular nature of the independent artist most worked alone, producing work exclusive of one another.

At Bovard Studio groups of artists are organized to collaborate and combine forces as a community on all projects. Through this experience I feel I have glimpsed the secret of the Renaissance and its rapid advancement of the arts. I am convinced when groups of artists cooperate and work together every day on project after project, their artistic skills and talents grow and flourish far more rapidly than one would have thought possible when working individually. It has been an amazing inspiration to watch the synergistic growth of our artists.

Much of the success of Bovard Studio's artists can be attributed to the fact that we do not limit our search to experienced glass painters for our art department. In fact glass painting experience is not even considered an asset. Instead we look for talented and creative artists and teach them to paint on glass. When a brilliant artist learns a new medium, the result is brilliant art. It only stands to reason that it is far more difficult, and rare, for a mediocre artist to become a great painter than for a great artist to learn a new medium.

One of the primary motivations behind Bovard Studio's development of our Life of Christ scenes and Religious Symbol Medallions (see pages 20 to 24), was to create a training program for our new artists to learn and practice the unfamiliar medium of glass painting. They establish their new found skills by painting hundreds of pieces of the same art glass scene. This repetition allows them to master the medium of glass painting in an efficient, economical, and productive way.

Bovard Studio has a number of wholesale distributors that supply a standardized line of hand painted Medallion Scenes to the independent glass studios in the United States, Canada, Europe, Japan, Africa and South America. In addition many of these studios also order custom and original art glass painting directly from Bovard Studio for their religious and other art glass projects.

Many people have asked me how Bovard Studio became so successful in such a short period of time. One major ingredient is that I love my work. For any business to succeed in the long term, you must have a passion for what you are doing. Statistics have shown that the success rate for new businesses is very low. Unless you start with outside capital, you may have to work for very little money. Oftentimes, you must pay for the privilege of working in your chosen field for up to three years. This is because most or all of the income generated by the new business must be reinvested back into the business for it to develop and grow. The bottom line is, it's important to select a business you love enough to work at for very little money, often for free, and sometimes at a loss, until you get established. The large majority of new businesses fail within the first three years, so all you may end up with is the joy you had from the effort. As long as you show up and put in a full day's work you are still in business. The longer you do this, the more your chances for success increase.

When I started as an independent artist in 1971, I struggled to make a living as a fine artist, a painter. I had considerable success exhibiting my work in museums and galleries across the U.S. and Europe, including one man shows at some prestigious New York City galleries. I received many approving reviews of my art work in newspapers and magazines and had my work selected for publication in several art books. (See page 157) This was a superb boost for my creative ego but did little to support a growing family which included my loving wife and five children. I managed to sell a substantial amount of art work, but at the end of the year there was far too little difference between the amount of income from gross sales and the expenses incurred to produce those sales.

It took some time for me to recognize that the system is heavily stacked against the artist, as it is in few other businesses. A survey conducted several years ago by the periodical Art Business News, revealed that 90% of the art sold in the United States is categorized as

A rendering for a new window to match the historic style of existing stained glass windows installed in a Catholic church in Indiana.

Easter Lily Window at First United Presbyterian Church.

A simple contemporary cross design for a very large window .

"traditional". My circumstantial observation is that the vast majority of artists graduating from art schools in the United States are contemporary artists, yet contemporary art comprises only 10% of the market. To top it all off, I was a contemporary artist.

An additional obstacle is the gallery system. There is huge competition among artists to be exhibited by reputable art galleries through which an artist's work is sold, and his or her reputation is established. The standard practice and requirement for artists is to supply the galleries with their art on a consignment basis. This means the gallery has no financial risk in inventory, leaving the artist to support the gallery with their artwork and assume most of the risk. Many times the artist is expected to pay for other expenses as well, such as framing and some advertising costs. On top of all this, most galleries take 50% to 60% commissions on the gross sale amount of the art. These terms, combined with the overabundance of artists willing to submit to them, have left very few artists in a position to make a reasonable living from their art work.

I had experimented with glass art as early as 1970. In 1982 I took a job as the art director for a company which had developed and patented the process for laser cutting of glass and support systems for abrasive water-jet cutting of glass. It was my duty to develop art and viable products for this new technology to produce. I gained valuable experience working with teams of high caliber engineers developing these technologies for glass cutting. Most of the art work we produced was computer aided design (CAD) which was in early development at that time. Being no computer whiz I was always selected as the "test dummy" to see if the systems the engineers developed were user friendly.

One of my strengths is that I have always been an enthusiastic individual. My contagious enthusiasm has always helped me to sell my work and selling the new products we developed came naturally to me. As it turned out, I was the most successful sales person in the company. I was continually getting pushed more and more into sales and eventually became the sales manager. The drawback was that I was doing less and less art work and realizing I was no longer doing what I loved to do, I made a decision to move on and resume my career as a full-time fine artist. Fortunately, my compensation at this company included a stock package and I was able to sell my stock to procure enough capital to start over again.

Shortly after I left that company, one of the manufacturer's representatives asked me to develop and manufacture a product line of stained glass for the door and window industry. The idea was to distribute these windows through lumber yard chains and home supply stores. For many months I declined, as my plan was to return to being a fine art painter who also worked in the medium of stained glass.

As fate would have it by January of 1986 I had hit rock bottom financially. The next time this representative called to make the same request again, I said yes. With much urgency in his voice he informed me that he needed the product line developed and the initial stocking order produced and shipped within 30 days. I told him it would take me at least 30 days to raise the capital before I could even start the project. He asked me how much capital I needed, I gave him a number, and the very next morning I received a check from him via Federal Express for the full amount I had quoted. The rest as they say is history and Bovard "Art Glass" Studio was born.

Fortunately I already had a large studio space in an old factory that had been converted into about 30 artist's studios. Having the facilities, I designed the product line, hired several craftspeople, built jigs, set up a production system and shipped out several hundred octagon stained glass window inserts 30 days later.

I should state at this point that I feel I had an advantage over many people in that I grew up in a family of entrepreneurs. My father had a small business, plus I had uncles and great uncles with small businesses. My wife also grew up in a family of business people. Her father had four businesses during his lifetime, and her maternal grandfather had a very successful large business. So as children both my wife and I witnessed first hand the risks and rewards of business. We lived through the ups and downs, the difficult times, and watched as perseverance turned failures into successes. Both of us were well aware of the swing and cadence of a small business before I started Bovard Studio. A supportive spouse and family is essential in any small business venture because the downs always go along with the ups.

By the end of 1986 we had landed several additional window insert accounts and our production department was in full swing. During that time we continued to develop our custom art glass division and had completed several smaller commissions, but more importantly we successfully completed our first church window commission. Over the next two years our custom business grew and by the end of 1988 it was clear to me that Bovard Studio's future was in architectural and ecclesiastic windows. I made a decision to concentrate our efforts in that direction.

I wrote to my production stained glass customers and gave them permission to use our copyrighted product lines which I had developed exclusively for them. I included a list of other art glass companies who would be more than happy to accept the accounts. Within a few months we filled our last production orders and we were out of the production business. We were now 100% committed to architectural stained glass. Our target markets would be churches, courthouses, libraries, museums, state government buildings, military bases, restaurants, and hotels. I was exhilarated to be moving forward into this

An example of the first production window inserts using "24k gold plated" leaded glass windows. We sold this product line through Lowes home supply centers.

A new memorial window to commemorate the California scientists who contributed to the World War II allied forces victory. Installed in the San Francisco, California War Memorial Veterans Building.

Installation view of twelve foot (3.66 m) diameter rose window for Church of the Ascension, Overland Park, Kansas.

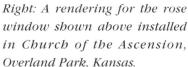

Right: A rendering for the rose window shown above installed in Church of the Ascension, Overland Park, Kansas.

new phase of business. Architectural glass was the most fulfilling thing I had ever been involved in and I am proud to say that we have been growing ever since.

One of the most important realities an entrepreneur must face is his or her own personal limitations. My experience as a child watching my father and uncles, helped me to see the importance of this lesson early on. So when the circumstance presented itself, I was mentally prepared to hire people who were more talented, with exceptional skills in areas I was lacking. For example our business manager and CFO (chief financial officer) has a strong accounting, banking and small business background with more than 25 years experience. He is one of the smartest businessmen I know. Our production director is a manufacturing engineer with a master's degree in business management with more than 30 years work experience. He is also a gifted Apostolic Catholic priest and bishop. We have several exceptionally talented and gifted artists and designers who run circles around my artistic limitations. Our training instructor for our stained glass fabricators has over 25 years experience and is one of the finest stained glass craftsmen that I know. He is a kind, patient and talented teacher who enthusiastically passes his talents on to new apprentices and helps our experienced craftspeople improve their skills.

I could go on listing the many qualities and special skills each person brings, suffice it to say that every one of our staff members has talents and gifts they bring with them everyday. As a bonus, this group of people are fun to be around. Needless to say, most have many other opportunities to practice their avocation, but they are here at Bovard Studio because they love what they are doing.

The Love of a Mother

THAT LUCKY SOUL whose life was spent in vocation, blissful duty to God, self and mankind is accepting of his fate. Better is life spent performing one's own vocation, no matter how lowly, than in that of another, as that brings great danger to life everlasting. Motherhood, the highest of vocations yet most common, lights the soul of mother. Individual love finds unity in the ocean of God's love. The love of mother for child is the purest of loves. It is love given freely from generation to generation with no expectations, no strings attached. It is mother giving heart, soul, and self, her essential being, pure, focused, concentrated love. This love flowing into baby's heart, nourishes this new life's soul. This love, though only a drop of concentrated individual love, gives us a glimpse of the ocean of God's love, omnipresent, eternal. Unifying bliss, I am That, Thou art That, all of manifest creation is That. All that is lacking are the eyes of the enlightened saved souls to see it. This is pure bliss consciousness, the one true vocation of every man, woman and child blessed with God's highest gift, life as a human being. No drop of precious love is lost as it merges with the ocean of God's love. Love, the treasure of the universe, flows between mother and child, an invincible force of nature, in the highest of holy vocations, motherhood.

A simple mother, Denise of Dallas, Texas, her body filled with cancer, is told by the finest doctors that she is going to die. Time, precious time, has run out. Planning her burial, she pursues one precious thought, her love for her three young daughters. Denise commissions a stained glass window.

Detail of the memorial window showing a guardian angel.

A MOTHER'S LOVE

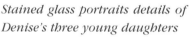

Stained glass portraits details of Denise's three young daughters

Those gifted artists who are fortunate enough to work in this translucent medium of stained glass share a special knowledge. They understand that it is the light passing through the glass that is the art. Without the light, stained glass is nothing more than a drab and shadowy surface interlaced with a matrix of lead cames. Add the light, and it is possible to see the soul of man shining in the silhouette of God. – R. B.

She plans with Bovard Studio artists a window with her three young daughters playing in the garden. They are swinging among the clouds with their guardian angel's ever protecting conduit of an absent mother's love. The angel hovers over their blissful play, protecting innocent pure hearts, their treasured mother's love an eternal, precious drop in the ocean of God's love.

Defying her doctors', modern day sages, certain predictions, Denise clings to life, waiting the months it takes to see the stained glass window she has commissioned as she painstakingly helps the artists design every detail. In Fairfield, Iowa, Bovard Studio's artists create line by line, glass cut by glass cut, brush stroke by brush stroke, fired indelibly into the stained glass by the tongues of fire in Bovard Studio's gas fired kilns. A glimpse of precious mother's love is captured for time immemorial.

After the final pieces of stained glass are assembled, cradled in their lead cames, Bovard Studio's craftsmen place the final touches on the stained glass in the Dallas mausoleum, Denise's final resting place. Denise arrives with her loving husband and three precious loves. Tears flow freely as she sees her vision is realized. She returns home, to her vocation, a mother's life lived, her soul with all its precious love joins the ocean of God's love.

As we turn around to leave Denise's final resting place, directly across from her memorial stained glass window lies the new grave of Mickey Mantle. Autographed baseballs are piled there by teammates and rivals who stop by to pay their final respects.

When the client-artist trust relationship is in place, artistic license is granted to the artist to make changes and refinements during the process of designing, developing, and building a stained glass window. Often while the glass is being cut or laid out the artist will have an insight for a refinement that will add greater beauty to the finished window. Placing restrictions on this artistic license does not allow for artistic intuition to occur or for artistic genius to manifest itself.

Memorial window for a dying mother, reveals her ascending spirit and a guardian angel keeping watch over her three young daughters. Artist: Lyn Durham.

Religious Medallions

HAND-PAINTED MEDALLIONS, BORDERS AND ROSETTES

Stained and decorative glass suffered a steep decline in public interest from the mid 1940's to the early 1960's. The trend in new church buildings was for minimal decoration, with little or no stained glass in the windows. Tiffany lamps had gone out of style and many were thrown out with the trash (those same original Tiffany lamps would now be worth many thousands or even millions of dollars). It became fashionable to use plastics for color and decoration in the home. This was the era when many people decried that stained glass was a dead or dying art form.

The 1960's saw the beginning of a revival for the stained glass craft. The pop culture of the mid 60's exploded onto the scene with it's bold, confident designs and art glass became "cool" to a new generation of Americans. An art medium that used light and color to compose a work of art, was a natural connection to empower the self-expression of the "hip generation".

*Traditional Apostle
Luke Medallion*

Baptism Medallion

Custom Design Medallion

*Traditional Apostle
John Medallion*

Communion Medallion

*Apostle John Medallion
shown installed in window*

20

Hand-Painted Medallions

During the 1970's, proponents and neophyte crafters were attracted to this age-old art form and the revival was truly underway. Small art glass studios were established and artistic experimentation was rampant. Hobby instruction classes were offered everywhere you looked and glass crafting flourished as a do-it-yourself art. New glass manufacturing facilities were born and older established glass factories "rediscovered" lost formulas for making unusual and diverse types of stained glass. It wasn't long before glass, very similar to the type L. C. Tiffany & Co. used at the turn of the century, was readily available.

While there were hundreds of studios now at work producing beautiful stained glass works, one aspect of the art, painting on glass, was trailing behind the progress made in the art glass craft as a whole. Most studios developed and refined their skills as stained glass artists but did not include glass painting in their repertories. Perhaps this was due to a lack of qualified instruction or to difficulty in obtaining the specialized stains and other supplies. Whatever the reason, the scarcity of glass painters turned out to be a golden opportunity for Bovard Studio.

In the late 1990's we recognized there was a need for ready-made glass components with traditional hand-painted motifs, which could be incorporated into stained glass windows. We developed several prototypes of glass medallions, featuring both religious and secular painted designs then made a presentation to one of our trusted suppliers. We showed them our samples and explained the concept of offering authentic hand-painted stained glass medallions to the rapidly growing number of professional and hobby-craft artisans. To our delight, the distributor said yes and we left with a purchase order. Our elegant hand-painted glass products are now carried by most art glass distributors and are available through thousands of stained glass retailer supply stores around the world.

Traditional St. Michael Medallion

Traditional Apostle Mark Medallion

Bible & Cross Medallion

Vine & Branches Medallion

Jesus Knocking - with an optional
painted border cluster set.

Blessing the Children

Ascension

Baptism

Resurrection at the Tomb

Madonna and Child

Jesus Walking on the Water

The Good Shepherd

Gethsemane

Bovard Studio's custom medallions include eighteen hand-painted and kiln-fired "Life of Christ" and "Old Testament" scenes. These Medallions are available in 18" x 24" (45.7 x 61 cm) oval, 18" x 24" (45.7 x 61 cm) rectangle and 18" x 24" (45.7 x 61 cm) royal arch shapes. Also available are 12" x 16" (30.5 x 40.6 cm) oval, 12" x 16" (30.5 x 40.6 cm) rectangle and 12" x 16" (30.5 x 40.6 cm) royal arch shapes, along with 9" and 12" (22.8 & 30.5 cm) circles (disk shape). These medallions look great with a simple border added to hang as an autonomous panel or

Nativity

Feeding the Multitude

The Last Supper

Head of Christ

Crucifixion

Annunciation

The Ten Commandments

Daniel and the Lions

Noah's Ark

they can be incorporated into full-size, custom designed leaded glass windows with borders and a geometric background. See an example on page pg 132 and dozens more in the Design Gallery on pages 104 to 139.

BORDERS

BORDERS AND ROSETTES are painted with tracing black pigment that is kiln-fired onto a colored background glass. These components were used extensively in older liturgical and domestic stained glass windows and continue to be used for many traditional designs today. The pattern repeats and matches as it traces around the perimeter of the window. The rosettes are used to anchor the corners or may be interlaced into the border depending on the artist's concept.

The Life of Christ series windows on pages 8, 128 & 129 are fine examples of how these components may be used in a stained glass window design.

NOTE: These hand painted Borders, Rosettes and our Medallion Symbol series (pages 20 - 23) are available worldwide from many retail distributors.

Border components with floral & fauna motifs

Border components with geometric motifs

ROSETTES

Rosette components with floral and geometric motifs

Left: New building addition at The Sacred Heart Church, Boulder, Colorado, showing the location of new stained glass windows commissioned to match the style of their original windows.

New stained glass windows using hand painted medallions were custom designed to compliment existing windows for The Sacred Heart Church in Boulder, Colorado.

The Descending Dove (above right) is a standard medallion design. Pietà (above) is a custom medallion created especially for The Sacred Heart Church in Boulder, Colorado.

5

GOD'S TEST OF FAITH

God's Challenge

A window from the United Methodist Church, Hamilton, Illinois after modification, restoration and installation into the new church.

DEEP RUMBLING THUNDER shakes the ancient bedrock under the new brick building of the United Methodist Church in Hamilton, Illinois. Lightning illuminates the dark evening sky as primal forces rain water and fire down upon the earth. In a sudden flash, bricks fly and timbers burst into flames. This night is to become another one of God's challenges, a test of faith for this young congregation.

Church members and neighbors are instantaneously roused from their homes and without hesitation spring into action. Men and women rush into the burning building, some rescue the new organ from the flames while others recover the pews, setting them safely into the wet grass a safe distance away. A few of the faithful climb upon the over-heated brick walls, rushing trust before personal safety and pull each and every stained glass window from the burning building. Newspaper records of the incident from 1905 reported that "hot molten lead dripped down arms of rescuers, searing their flesh".

This Methodist congregation was first organized in 1853 on the east bank of the mighty Mississippi River just south of Navoo. On this day in 1905 the Methodist faithful are simultaneously devastated and blessed in God's firm hands, symbolized by their newly tempered souls standing before the smoldering embers of the now destroyed four year old brick church building.

Members of the church risked their lives to save the glass from the heat of the flames. A newspaper story preserved from that period reports that hot lead ran down the arms of rescuers who retrieved all windows intact. One can easily surmise that of utmost importance in the construction of our new facility was the continued use of the stained glass windows. - Excerpt of letter from Pastor Paul Smit, Hamilton United Methodist Church, Hamilton, Illinois.

The entrance lobby at United Methodist Church showing some of the modified windows incorporated into the new building.

A new challenge has arrived for the forever faithful and like the Phoenix this church shall rise again. It was rebuilt in 1910 on the same foundation of the recently destroyed church and the courageously rescued stained glass windows would be incorporated into the new church building.

Time passes along as surely as the ever-flowing Mississippi. By 1987, old age has beset this once proud building. The practical 1980's.what to do? The cost of utilities, maintenance and repair exceeds the cost of a mortgage on a new building that would better serve the needs of today's congregation.

The decision is made to build a new modern church. Money is raised and plans are set but not before the heritage of their ancestors is taken to heart. Those stained glass windows, saved so many years ago by faithful souls must not be cast aside. Could they be redesigned and incorporated into the new building? With the help of Bovard Studio, their precious heritage now rests in the restored stained glass windows that will easily last another 100 years and beyond.

One unique feature of our old building was that every window was stained glass. Along with the beauty the windows provided, was a heritage that gave the glass even greater value. In the early 1900's the church burned shortly after the initial construction was completed. - Excerpt of letter from Pastor Paul Smit, Hamilton United Methodist Church.

Incorporating Historic Glass

SALVAGING HISTORY

These chapel windows in the Trinity Episcopal Cathedral in Davenport, Iowa, incorporates salvaged stained glass sections into a simple diamond background.

THE HISTORIC TRINITY EPISCOPAL CATHEDRAL in

Davenport, Iowa decided to build a new chapel. The Cathedral had previously acquired several antique stained glass windows from an Anglican church in England. The Cathedral's building committee asked Bovard Studio to incorporate these historic windows into five large new window frames set into their newly constructed chapel. We found the windows stacked on top of each other, lying on a bare cement floor next to the furnace. Needless to say they had suffered heavy damage from careless handling and storage and had significant breakage including the painted faces of several figures.

We decided the best solution was to deconstruct the windows and incorporate the surviving design elements into the new windows. We started by placing the faces of angels in the center section of the 'rose tracery' at the top of each of the five window frames. We used some of the original angel sections from the salvaged stained glass and our painting department replicated some angels as needed.

Left two photos: Salvaged fragments from an old English window prior to cleaning and restoration. These have been incorporated into the new chapel windows at Trinity Episcopal Cathedral.

The next step was to disassemble the antique stained glass panels. Our goal was to preserve as much of the original glass design in the antique windows as possible. We laid the original glass pieces on the working drawing and replicated any broken and/or missing glass pieces, including several faces and flesh areas. The design team incorporated the figurative sections from the historic stained glass panels into the center two lancets of the stained glass windows. The design was brought into balance by expanding the design from the center lancets to allow it to flow into the outside lancets using imagery appropriate to the themes of the figures in the historic style. We pushed a few painted panes of stained glass from the design of the two center lancets into the clear diamond lights of the outside lancets and filled the balance of the space with the diamond shaped lights of clear mouth blown antique glass. We added several clear faceted jewels and tied the design together with a simple border of mouth blown red antique glass.

The outcome was delightful. These five large stained glass windows flood this traditionally designed chapel with clear light and a smattering of prismatic rainbows from the faceted jewels that move across the worship space with the sun. The restored stained glass designs from the English Anglican church feature scenes of The Good Shepherd, Christ Feeding the Multitude, and Christ in the Temple, to remind worshippers of the timeless accounts of Christ's life.

Above: This chapel window, from Trinity Episcopal Cathedral in Davenport, Iowa, incorporates salvaged stained glass sections into a simple diamond background. It's an excellent example of how mullions are used to break a large window opening into smaller sections. The four large lower sections plus the decorative tracery mullions in the upper section add interest and intrigue to the overall design.

We Have Our Own Artist

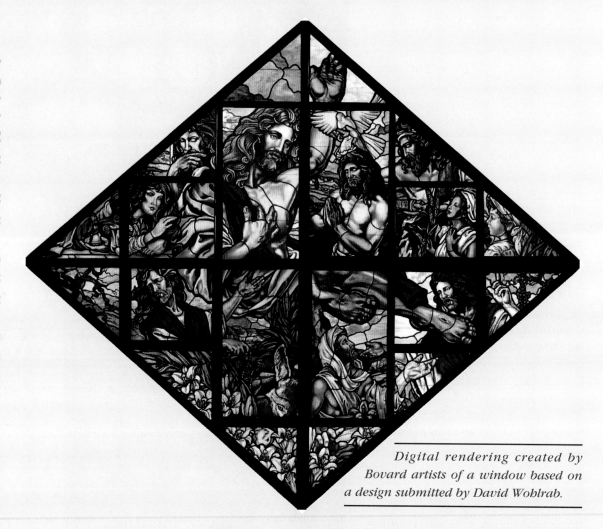

Digital rendering created by Bovard artists of a window based on a design submitted by David Wohlrab.

I HEAR IT FROM CLIENTS several times per year "We have an artist on our committee who has created a design for our new stained glass window". Generally what we get are sketches or paintings that are inspired but regrettably created with little artistic talent. Bethany Lutheran Church in Naperville, Illinois was an exception. They have a talented professional artist, David Wohlrab, in their congregation who volunteered to design their new stained glass window. His figurative window design, titled "Soli Deo Gloria (To God Alone Be The Glory)", has dynamic movement and flow that can be described as contemporary elegance with a classical feel. Our glass painters and craftspeople created a remarkable stained glass window that was produced faithfully from the rendering and artistic input of Bethany Lutheran's talented artist.

David Wohlrab's figurative design, titled "Soli Deo Gloria", has a dynamic style that can be described as contemporary elegance with a classical feel.

Final installation showing the window above the entrance doors at the back of the sanctuary.

Undoubtedly, volunteer artists and/or decorators have the best interest of the project at heart. The window committee appoints one of their creative members to guide and assist the glass studio and to contribute artistically in any way possible. Unfortunately the assistance of a non-glass designer can sometimes muddle a project. The art of stained glass is rooted in what happens to the light as it passes through the stained glass window. An understanding of this complexity is essential. Our experience has been that non-glass designers inevitably select the glass based on what colors match this or that element within the interior design of the church without considering the fact that light itself must be the dominant feature. A matching color scheme is one matter but if the effect of the light is downplayed the result can be a nondescript or melancholy atmosphere within the worship space.

Precise glass selection is paramount to prevent major problems such as glare from east or south facing stained glass windows. Lack of contrasting density and colors can produce a confusing interpretation for the viewer of the stained glass window. When light is not the dominant feature we are left with an abstract space with no visible content.

Bethany Lutheran Church in Naperville, Illinois formed a committee to commission a stained glass window for the sanctuary.

Our experience with Bethany Lutheran was extraordinary. We wholeheartedly acknowledged David Wohlrab as the talented designer that he is and he accepted our expertise as stained glass artists and craftspeople. Our staff selected the proper glass, used their talented glass painting and assembly techniques and transformed David's inspired vision into an exceptional stained glass heritage that will inspire many generations of Bethany Lutheran Church's worshippers.

WEST ANGELES CATHEDRAL PROJECT

A Monumental Project

THE UNDERTAKING TO DESIGN AND FABRICATE the stained glass for this monumental project was one of Bovard Studio's greatest challenges. Not only did we have to design a stained glass heritage for this great congregation, but also we had to have it approved by the City of Los Angeles to meet their stringent earthquake codes.

Mrs. Mae Blake, an interior designer by profession, was charged with the task of decorating the new West Angeles Cathedral. There seemed to be no end to the energy that Mrs. Blake put into her responsibility that included approval of the stained glass window design. Mrs. Blake worked closely with our design team that included Sándor Fehér, Tess Bovard-Sachs, Anna McKnight and Roseveta Kantcheva. Together they discussed and exchanged many concepts, ideas and design renderings for the West Angeles stained glass that was ongoing for close to a year. Everyone involved had a strong desire to create the best legacy of art glass possible. The effort included a trip by Mrs. Blake and her husband Bishop Charles E. Blake to our studio in Fairfield, Iowa. The entire design team plus other experts from our staff, sat down to review the many design concepts and renderings at our disposal, to refine and come to a decision on a final design. After several hours of brainstorming we were tantalizingly close to a selection, but the Blake's still had reservations.

We were swiftly closing in on the launch date to begin construction of the stained glass in order to comply with the strict construction schedules. This project was special in many ways. The stained glass was more than a decorative element that could be installed in the building at a later date (as most stained glass can be). This building was in an earthquake zone and the construction of the stained glass windows had become an integral part of the curtain wall structure of the building itself in order to meet the code. Consequently the stained glass had to be completed on time or the construction of the entire building could suffer a significant delay or worse, come to a complete stop.

Desperate to solve the design impasse, I flew to Los Angeles to see if I could assist the project team to arrive at a suitable design before time ran out. Needless to say everyone involved was highly motivated to find a solution. However we were not willing to settle for less than the absolute best design to compliment the architectural integrity of the building and the inspired aspirations of the congregation.

Left: This design, titled 'The Holy Spirit', was selected and approved for the central panel of a 108' (32.9 m) high steeple tower that is a prominent feature at the front of the cathedral.

A collage of renderings showing various exterior views and window details of the approved design titled 'The Holy Spirit' for the West Angeles Cathedral in Los Angeles, California.

Above: Bishop Charles E. Blake, Teresa Bovard-Sachs (project manager) and Ron Bovard (President of Bovard Studio) celebrate the completion of the stained glass project for West Angles Cathedral. Photo by: Ramon Mentor

Below: West Angles Cathedral is complete and adorned with the new stained glass windows. Photo by: Ricky Brown.

We spent a long day reviewing the numerous design options that were the fruit of months of intense focus by the Bovard Studio design team and Mrs. Blake. It was after dark and we were sitting with Mrs. Blake in her office at Elegant Interiors. We had dozens of attractive concepts before us but not one stood out with that special spark that we all felt was essential for this project. I suggested that we start afresh, with a box of magic markers, scissors and a glue stick to compose some impulse collages and drawings, looking for that moment of inspiration. We were not disappointed; within a short period of time a concept with an inspirational spark was divinely conveyed. The seed had been planted that would eventually grow into the 'Holy Spirit' window, with a myriad of colors that Bishop Blake identified as an emblem of diversity.

Back in our studio, Sándor spent many long hours converting and expanding our small conceptual sketch into a beautiful rendering that encompassed the entire suite of stained glass for the new West Angeles Cathedral.

We had the design and a loose concept of colors but we still had one more essential challenge for a successful stained glass project; the actual glass selection. We sent a series of glass sample sets to Mrs. Blake and we had many conversations regarding the qualities and possibilities of glass that would meet the color criteria.

Above: The right side view of the completed tower windows.

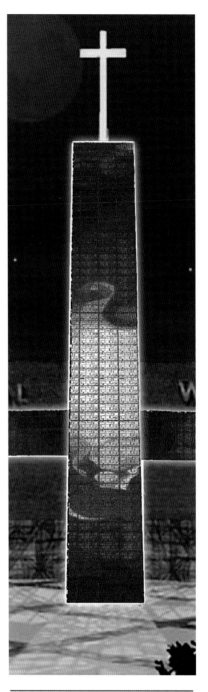

Above: One of several conceptual drawings submitted for the Cathedral project.

There was another serious consideration as well. The sheer size of this project would need a massive amount of glass to fabricate. When this is added to the accelerated schedule for completion of this project, we had no choice but to limit our glass selection to glass that was currently in stock and available in large quantities. In addition we needed to partner with a glass manufacturer that could make up any unexpected shortfalls caused by any reason, including disastrous breakage in shipping. Marita Findley, an executive at one of our chief glass suppliers was instrumental in this process. She recruited the full support of several art glass manufacturers for this large-scale project.

West Angeles Cathedral

The West Angeles Cathedral under construction in the Spring of 2000.

One of several conceptual illustrations that were submitted for the West Angeles Cathedral project.

The steeple tower alone was 10' (3.0 m) wide by 108' (32.9m) high. The clerestory horizontal band of stained glass was 8' (2.4m) high by 653' (199m) wide (more than the length of two football fields). It was obvious that we needed an immense quantity of glass and we needed it quickly.

I flew to Los Angeles once again to meet with Mrs. Blake and finalize the glass selection. We met in the offices of Elegant Interiors that sits directly across the street from the construction site of the new West Angeles Cathedral. By now the steel framework was nearing completion (see photo above left, of the structure taken by me on this very day) and time was running out.

We examined and compared the many possibilities. This project was to be viewed at night with backlighting as well as being a significant architectural daytime feature. Our task was to select glass that worked in sunlight, for the daylight view of the stained glass windows without imparting a negative color distortion that could show up when the stained glass windows were seen in artificial backlighting.

Opposite Page: The left side view of the completed tower windows. Photo by: Ricky Brown.

Translucent colored stained glass (a.k.a. cathedral glass) tends to appear as dark negative space during daylight hours, when viewed from the outside in reflected light. On the other hand opalescent glass (colored glass mixed with a white base) broadcasts its color in reflected light. If opalescent glass was used exclusively the sheer magnitude of color would overpower and dominate the exterior facade of the building. For this reason I ruled out the use of opalescent glass for the West Angeles Cathedral project. I settled on a combination of cathedral glass plus the restrained use of wispy stained glass for selected areas. Wispy stained glass is a mixture of translucent glass color with a subtle swirl (a wisp) of white and other milky opalescent colors scattered throughout the sheet of stained glass.

These double doors open into the steeple tower vestibule allowing an awesome view of the stained glass panels that rise 108' (32.9m) overhead. See photo on next page (at top left) for a view looking up from inside the tower .

The impact is subtle as compared to opalescent glass where the entire sheet of stained glass has an opalescent base of white mixed with the selected translucent colors. All of this brightly colored stained glass was balanced by using broad abstract bands of black opaque glass to provide structure to the finished design of the 'Holy Spirit' stained glass window.

This produced the desired effect in reflected daylight that complimented the building's architecture and exhibited the essence of the windows' design and color during the day.

The final piece to this monumental puzzle was to devise a system to fabricate these panels using a process of laminating the stained glass to a base of 1/2" (13 mm) thick laminated tempered glass. This process had been in use for several decades and had already been tested for severe wind load and approved to meet the stringent codes imposed by Dade County, Florida after Hurricane Andrew. The City of Los Angeles

Above: One of several conceptual illustrations that were submitted for the West Angeles Cathedral project.

Above: Greg Bovard with one of the completed panels ready for installation in the upper windows that circle the sanctuary. Note the large rack on wheels to help us move these heavy panels around.

approved our use of this combination of products to meet earthquake codes. We were ready to go and everything looked great until the architect informed us that the basic stained glass panel sizes would have to be 10 ft. (3.1 m) wide by 8 ft. (2.4 m) high. These panels were three times the size of previous panels made with these techniques.

We contracted with a company to supply the lamination materials, the equipment and training for our staff. They assured us that we would not have a problem fabricating panels of this size. We paid their company expert to come to Los Angeles and get us started on the project. Over the course of 2 days we ran several tests trying in vain to coax the laminating material to completely fill the space between the stained glass and the base layer of 1/2" (13 mm) thick laminated tempered glass. Unfortunately these initial tests failed and the only solution the expert could offer was to downsize the panels to less than

half the size as those we were required to fabricate. This solution was unacceptable.

We were faced with construction deadlines that carried severe penalties and liabilities for delays, so the pressure was on. My daughter Tess was the project manager and she decided, along with my son Greg and three other staff members, that a solution had to be found – and quickly! With support and suggestions from our two staff engineers, Tess and her team started a series of experiments on their own. It took some trial and error but within a few days they had developed a unique and proprietary series of techniques that resulted in the successful fabrication of the required full size panels.

It took many prayers by our friends at West Angeles along with a measure of divine intervention to realize the successful completion of West Angeles Cathedral's new stained glass heritage. Our client was thrilled with the results and we even found enough time to fabricate some additional stained glass panels for the backside of the tower above the roofline.

Opposite Page, Bottom: All panels for the upper windows that circle the sanctuary are complete and installed, Here our crew is installing the last few panels at the top of the tower.

Above: Installation of panels in the steeple tower. We used a hydraulic platform (seen in the lower left corner) and a truck-mounted crane with platform to lift and position each panel.

DESIGN DEVELOPMENT

The first step in creating a stained glass window is to determine the desire of the church congregation, usually through consultation with an art window committee. It is the designer's task to interpret the clients desire for expression of faith, history, or aspirations within the chosen artistic style. They will set aside sufficient time to discuss the project in detail, exchanging ideas using photographs, drawings, and sketches until a concept is revealed. The designer will then prepare a color proposal rendering for presentation, after which refinements will be made until a final design is agreed upon.

GLASS SELECTION

One of the most significant stages in the creation of a stained glass window is glass selection. There are literally thousands of different colors, textures and densities of glass available today. The designer will select the glass for the various areas of the window coinciding with the final approved color rendering and make the final decisions for the colors and textures.

GLASS PAINTING

Not all stained glass windows have painted details. Depending on the design style chosen, a window may require painting to define border and/or background details. If the design is figurative, painting will be necessary to add realistic details to the faces, hands, and clothing. After the glass has been cut and shaped into the various component pieces, the artist applies the paint, using traditional glass "stains", mat blending colors, and colored enamels. This process of "staining" the glass is where the term "stained glass" comes from.

ASSEMBLY AND FABRICATION

After every glass component has been cut, shaped, and painted it is time to assemble or "lead up" the stained glass window. Usually the designer will make one final inspection of the window arranged on a light table or glass easel to view it exactly as it will be assembled. Once satisfied, the fabricator begins the leading process by stretching an "H" channel strip of lead (called a "came"), then placing it on the assembly drawing along one outside edge of the window. The first glass piece is positioned and temporarily held with a tack nail. Another lead strip is cut, shaped and positioned; then the second, adjoining glass piece is arranged into the assembly. This operation continues until every component is in place. The final step in the assembly process is to solder the lead strips together at each joint, to hold the stained glass window together.

CEMENTING AND CLEANING

This important process will stiffen and strengthen the leaded panels, making them weather tight. The glazing cement or putty is pushed into the space between the flanges of the lead came and the glass, on both sides of the window. Then the excess is cleaned off with a special compound called "whiting", leaving the glass clean and imparting an aesthetically pleasing dark "patina" on the surface of the lead came.

INSTALLATION

When the window is complete, the client will be contacted to set an appointment for installation of the new stained glass window. This is a crucial final step and it must be performed by qualified installers who understand the requirements for reinforcing. If exterior protective glazing was specified for the window, it should be installed at this time as well.

New Stained Glass Windows

DESIGN DEVELOPMENT PROCESS

WHEN A CLIENT WANTS a new stained glass window, the first and most important step is to listen carefully to the client's request. Of course, we must also consider the architectural space, adjoining windows, building style, light source intensity and direction, and any trees, buildings, mountains, or other obstacles that may block the available light. All these variables must be taken into account during the process of forming the core concept but in the end it all comes down to fulfilling the client's desire.

Left: New windows being designed by Sándor Fehér using a computer to create a rendering of the finished art glass as it would look in the building after installation.

In the not too distant past we would render our design proposal as a watercolor painting or use colored dyes on transparent film to illustrate our concept for the client's approval. Today we create our proposal rendering using our computer aided design (CAD) system. It takes our artists about the same length of time to create a digital rendering as it did to produce a watercolor painting. However with a digital design, we don't have to start over if the client wants to make changes. Now changes to the proposal, even major ones, such as a complete color makeover or a proportion adjustment are made quickly and simply, allowing us to communicate with our client graphically in a way they can understand. It is our responsibility to demystify the process for our clients.

A proposal rendering created with a computer aided design (CAD) system for a Georgia Performing Art Center. The 3-D views of the proposal renderings show how they would appear after installation into the building.

An easy way to experience the contrast of transmitted light is to look at a familiar church window from the outside during the day – you'll notice a very dramatic difference.

The client may also need some guidance to help them understand the unique nature of stained glass as a "transmitted light" medium. If you look at a stained glass window in reflected light (from the same side as the light source), you will find yourself looking at a relatively dark surface, with a few light colored opalescent (milky) glass areas. An easy way to experience this is to look at a familiar church window from the outside during the day – you'll notice a dramatic difference. Even the opalescent glass areas have a very different, less interesting characteristic in reflected light.

This is an example of a "transmitted light" interior view of the Good Shepherd window in United Presbyterian Church of Morning Sun, Iowa.

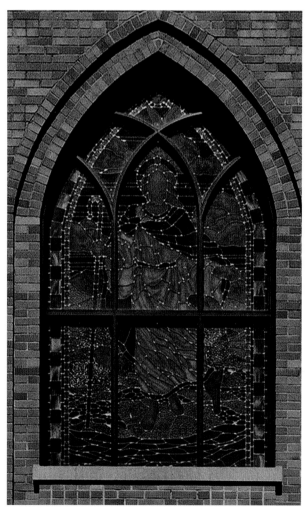

This is the same window (as on the left) viewed from the outside during daylight in "reflected light". The contrast is dramatic.

This brings us back to the rendering. A proposal rendered on paper, by its very nature, is presented in a medium of reflected light. At best, it can only give the client an indication of how the finished stained glass will look. Even a proposal prepared on transparent film, which is a medium of transmitted light (similar to stained glass), cannot portray the depth and richness of stained glass. Very few clients are able to visualize the overall effect of the glass in the finished window even when colored glass samples are presented along with the rendering. For this reason, it is very important to establish a trust relationship between the client and the stained glass artist.

The most innovative and poetic work is accomplished by allowing an experienced artist the creative freedom to visualize. Of course the artist must stay within the clients' established design boundaries as well as other considerations such as correctness of religious symbols, liturgy, architectural styles, and artistic style factors such as modern, traditional, abstract, representational, etc.

The most innovative and poetic work is accomplished by allowing an experienced artist the creative freedom to visualize.

A computer rendering that has been approved by the customer (notice signature in lower right). This color image will serve as a guide throughout the production of the window.

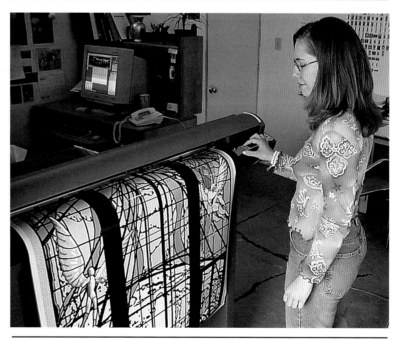

Ron's daughter Tess Bovard-Sachs, a designer and project manager, is shown here printing a poster sized proposal on the ENCAD system color plotter.

11

Colors & Fabrication

WHEN THE CLIENT AND ARTIST have settled on a design, the project is scheduled and full-size measurements and templates are taken. The artist begins by drafting a full-size pattern drawing consisting of the lead lines in the window.

Lead is the matrix that holds the dozens, hundreds or even thousands of colored glass pieces together in the finished window. A "leaded" glass window is fabricated using lead strips (called "cames") that are extruded in the shape of an "H". A window may use only one size of came or it may have several sizes and shapes to fulfill certain design effects. Artistically the lead lines create a negative space (areas not transmitting light) and the careful mix of negative and positive space is very important in any work of art.

Structural composition is the rudimentary element that determines how long a stained glass window will last. A large window will be fabricated in several independent sections that will be layered or stacked during installation into the window frame. Leaded glass windows should be limited to panel sections of 12 square feet (1.2 meters squared) or less. A competent designer must incorporate the structural requirements into the design, based on the window's size and proportion. If designed, fabricated and installed correctly a stained glass window will last for many generations.

Top: Laying out the lead lines of a pattern using a computer. Above: Our Pre-production engineer, Steve Henry, is printing a full-size pattern from the computer using a pen plotter.

M an has the power to create his own reality through the power of his consciousness. He can choose to live in the ever changing desert of temporal pleasures and suffering. If we simply go to The Kingdom of God within us all, we can connect to a pipeline that is ever flowing from the ocean of God's love, quenching the desert of temporal existence to make it bloom in spiritual bliss. - R. B.

Left: A "leaded" glass window is fabricated using lead strips (called "cames") that are extruded in the shape of an "H".

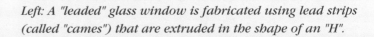

GLASS SELECTION AND FABRICATION

GLASS SELECTION

One of the most significant stages in the creation of a stained glass window is glass selection. We literally have thousands, close to 4,000 different colors, textures and densities of glass readily available today. The various types of stained glass range from translucent colors, called "cathedral glass" to semi-translucent "wispy" or "streaky" colored glass to an "opalescent" that has an opaque white base added to the color. It may be manufactured or "rolled" by machine or it may be hand-mixed and rolled by a small crew of glassmakers. Alternatively, it may be made mouth-blown by skilled artisans in the "antique" tradition. The varieties of glass you may encounter within these manufactured types are seedy (bubbles), crackle, flashed, reamy, and streaky glass. You will also find a variety of textures available such as ripple, baroque, granite, water, fibrillated, chipped, and many others.

To expand the available range of color, texture and density even further, American artists such as Louis Comfort Tiffany and John LaFarge devised a process called "plating" which they used extensively in their stained glass windows. A "plate" is a second layer of glass, added to a selected area within the window to create a new color or to increase the perception of depth. Some art glass windows fabricated by the L.C. Tiffany & Co. in the late 1800's & early 1900's have areas with up to seven plates on top of one another to achieve the artists' desired effect.

Just imagine, we have an assortment of more than 4,000 glass varieties available to us and placing two layers together theoretically expands the glass selection possibilities to a mind numbing 16,000,000. Those possibilities expand exponentially as more plate-layers are added. Of course, with each subsequent layer of plating, the glass density increases thereby lowering the transmitted light, so limitations do exist.

Types of stained glass range from translucent colors, called "cathedral glass" to semi-translucent "wispy" or "streaky" colored glass to an "opalescent" that has an opaque white base added to the color.

A careful examination of this photo of a restored Tiffany window reveals extensive use of plating. The arrows on the photo point out some of the multi-level plated areas.

We literally have thousands, close to 4,000 different colors, textures and densities of glass readily available today.

Julie Rickert, one of Bovard Studio's fabricators, is cutting glass for a new window project underway on her bench.

GLASS CUTTING AND SHAPING

Once the glass selection has been finalized and the full-size drawing is complete, it is time to select the actual glass sheets that will be cut into the component pieces for the window's design. The artist must carefully choose the ideal area of the colored glass sheet, taking into account the variations within the sheet, to achieve the desired artistic expression. As pieces are cut they are laid out on a light table, or a viewing easel. The easel is a sheet of clear glass that is positioned in front of a natural light window and the stained glass pieces are temporarily fixed onto it.using sticky wax. This way the artist can examine the effect of light passing through the stained glass composition. They will examine color, density, streak direction, texture, and any other aspect that may have an effect on the overall composition and make refinements and adjustments as necessary. When the client-artist trust relationship is in place, artistic license is granted to the artist to make changes and refinements during the process of designing, developing, and building a stained glass window. Often while the glass is being cut or laid out the artist will have an insight for a refinement that will add greater beauty to the finished window. Placing restrictions on this artistic license does not allow for artistic intuition to occur or for artistic genius to manifest itself.

The glass pieces are cut out, painted and waxed up on a glass easel or laid out on a light table to check the effect of light passing through the stained glass composition. Example shown is St. Boniface window for Christ the King Abbey, Cullman, Alabama.

GLASS PAINTING

While not all stained glass windows have painted details, a large percentage of ecclesiastic window designs do require some painting to define border and/or background details. Some designs, such as figurative, require painting to add realistic details to faces, hands, feet, and other design elements. After the glass has been cut and shaped into the various component pieces, the artist applies the paint, using traditional glass "stains", mat blending colors, and/or enamels. Most glass "stains" are made from heavy metal oxides. For instance gold will produce a red color, silver oxide produces yellow or gold, and cobalt yields a blue color. Many different oxides and paints are used to "stain the glass", depending on the desired color or effect.

The artist mixes the glass paints in a medium such as water, alcohol or oil, and includes a binder, glass frit and paint flux, depending on the formula for that particular stain. The artist laboriously grinds and mixes these components by hand with a muller or a palette knife until they have achieved the desired consistency.

Gold is used to create a red color on glass, silver oxide produces yellow or gold-amber, and cobalt yields a blue color. These and other heavy metal oxides are used to stain the surface of the glass for the desired color and effect. An interesting side note; this process of "staining" the glass is where the term "stained glass" comes from.

Yuriy Maltsev, one of Bovard Studio's glass painters, makes a final inspection of a completed face, just prior to turing it over to the fabrication department.

After the paint has been applied, artist Ilie Honkanen places the glass in a kiln to be "fired" and permanently bond the paint to the surface of the glass.

When painting a figurative piece, the first applied layer of paint consists of the tracing lines, usually black, applied with a sable "tracing" brush. After the tracing lines have been applied, the glass is "fired" in a kiln to permanently bond the paint to the surface of the glass. The next paint layer is called a mat (or matting) that requires a special blending brush hand-made from English badger hair. This light brownish mat paint is applied as a fine layer then blended with the badger brush to make it uniform and semi transparent. Once air-dried, this mat layer will be carefully brushed away (called lighting) by the artist to expose the areas that are to remain transparent. This stage of glass painting is the opposite of most painting practices. In this instance, the image is formed by lifting the paint off the matted surface of the glass. This matting process may be repeated a number of times, layering more mats over the first to create artistic depth and differentiation. Once the mat is to the artists satisfaction the glass is placed back into the kiln for a second firing to bond the mat layer to the glass surface. Depending on the design, there may be one or more final painting steps to apply more mats, opaque colors, additional stains or transparent enamels to the image. It will then be finished with one last kiln firing. A special note about kiln firing, the glass may be fired after each painting stage or it may be fired once with multiple layers of paint depending upon the artist's selected technique and preference.

SURFACE ETCHING A DESIGN

Surface etching is another technique that an artist may use to obtain contrasting colors within an individual piece of glass. A special type of glass called "flashed" is used for this process. Flashed glass is manufactured by applying a very thin layer of a darker color onto the surface of a lighter colored sheet of glass. The darker thin layer (the "flashed" layer) can be etched, engraved or sandblasted away to reveal areas of the lighter color underneath in whatever design is desired. For example, an artist may use a blue flashed on clear, then etch a design by removing some of the blue surface color to create a design of clear "stars" on a dark blue "sky" background.

FINAL INSPECTION

After every glass component has been cut, shaped, painted, etched or otherwise prepared, it is time to assemble or "lead up" the stained glass window. However, not before one final, and very important inspection is made. All finished glass components are arranged back on the light table, or fixed to the viewing easel, exactly as they will be assembled. The artist will make one final review of the work and make any desired adjustments and refinements.

Detail of a stained glass window showing an example of symbols etched out of red flashed glass. Detail from a window created for the Veterans' Administration Hospital, Knoxville, Iowa.

Lead Assembly

ASSEMBLY OR "LEADING-UP" THE WINDOW

Now the fabrication craftsperson takes over to assemble the stained glass window. The glass components are placed on the assembly bench and arranged on the working drawing according to the pattern lines.

The fabricator starts in one corner of the window and begins the leading process by stretching an "H" channel of lead came. It is important to stretch the lead prior to assembly to to tighten the molecular structure. Windows made from extruded lead that has not been properly stretched tend to sag and bulge prematurely. One lead strip is placed on the assembly drawing along the bottom and another strip along one side of the window. The first glass piece (usually a corner piece) is placed in this perimeter channel and temporarily held with a tack nail. Another piece of H lead is cut to size with a sharp lead knife or diagonal nipper pliers (called dykes) and shaped to fit around the exposed edge of the first glass piece.

A second, adjoining glass piece is placed in the perimeter channel and another lead strip is cut and placed along the exposed glass edge of that piece. This process continues along, placing glass, cutting and fitting lead strips, until every component is in place. The final step in the leading process is to solder the lead strips together at each joint creating one continuous metal matrix to hold the stained glass window together. The window is then turned over and soldered on the backside.

Modern lead came is extruded from a lead alloy which uses additives to enhance the tensile strength. Older lead came (and some still available) was made from pure lead through a milling process that stresses the came and shortens its life expectancy.

Left: Fabricator Julie Rickert cuts H lead came to size with a lead knife. Above: Llona Wagner is shaping the came to fit around the exposed edge of the glass pieces that are temporarily held in place with a push pin.

Rose Buford (at right) has finished cementing and whiting and is now brushing the panel to remove the waste material. On the left side of the photo other department staff are working on windows that have been placed in front of a light easel for final inspection and cleaning.

Rodger Haynes, uses a wood pick to remove any cement that has seeped out from under the flanges of the lead came. The pick is run around all edges of the lead came to cut and remove this excess.

CEMENTING AND CLEANING

The assembled window is now ready to be cemented. This important process will stiffen and strengthen the leaded panels, making them weather tight, and adding an aesthetically pleasing dark "patina" to the lead surface. The cement or putty is packed into the space between the flanges of the lead came and the glass on both sides of the window, then the excess is cleaned off with a compound call "whiting". There is division among stained glass professionals on the best formula for glazing cement; primarily, whether a hardener (such as plaster or Portland cement) should be added to the glazing formula or if an unaltered commercially produced glazing putty is best. We have found that Portland cement is corrosive to the lead came and over time the lime will leach out producing a haze bordering the lead came that is very difficult to remove. Due to these negative effects our studio does not use Portland cement in our glazing cement.

Another traditional formula for glazing cement contains lead oxide as a primary ingredient. Lead oxide in powder form is easily inhaled and since the human body absorbs four times as much lead into the bloodstream by inhalation than from ingestion, lead oxide is no longer used (see 'Safety and Environment' on next page).

The glazing cement formula that we use has calcium carbonate (a.k.a. whiting) as its primary ingredient. You may recognize this compound from some popular anti-acid medicines, as calcium carbonate is well known to relieve acid indigestion.

The glazing cement is pushed under the flanges of the stained glass window using a stiff bristle brush. The excess cement is cleaned off with whiting and another vigorous brushing. This cleans and polishes the stained glass while another ingredient in the glazing cement, lampblack (carbon), darkens the lead came leaving a rich patina that is neutral in the design of the stained glass window.

Once cemented and cleaned, the stained glass window needs to setup for a few days until the cement has hardened. Some of the cement will have seeped out from under the flanges of the lead came and a wood pick is used to run around all edges of the lead came to cut and remove this excess putty. The stained glass window is then placed on a light easel (in front of a window) or onto a light table for final inspection and cleaning.

NOTE: When a leaded window is to be installed without protective exterior glazing, industry conservation guidelines specify that it must be sealed in a specific way to safeguard against leaks. The window must be built using flat 'H' lead came, then the lead flanges are bent back slightly and the opened space is hand packed with a linseed oil based putty. The lead flanges are then pressed back down onto the glass and the excess putty is picked off. After whiting and cleaning, the window must be laid flat to allow the putty to cure for about 2 weeks.

SAFETY AND ENVIRONMENT IN THE STAINED GLASS STUDIO

Public concern over the safety of working with lead and the effects of lead in the environment has resulted in strict government regulation for the use, handling and disposal of lead. Stained glass windows are held together with lead came, lead based solder and many are stained with lead based paints. The increased awareness and government regulation have resulted in much improved health and safety procedures for our industry's craftspeople, our clients, and the environment.

Bovard employee's have had their blood lead levels tested on a regular basis since the 1980's. We have a professional training program conducted by registered nurses specializing in occupational health and safety issues to instruct our staff on lead safety. Breathing lead dust (lead oxide) has four times the absorption rate into the bloodstream as ingesting lead. For this reason our studio's environment is constantly monitored for safe air lead levels. We have been very pleased with our track record and whenever one of our craftspeople tests with an elevated level of lead, we have found the main cause is careless hygiene, i.e. not washing their hands prior to smoking or eating.

The monitoring of lead levels in the studio environment has shown the highest risk area of lead exposure is during the restoration of historic stained glass windows. The glazing cement packed between the layers of the lead came, the old paint on the sash may contain lead oxide and of course the lead came and solder that hold the stained glass windows together contains lead.

We have initiated several techniques to reduce and/or eliminate the lead levels in the air of our restoration department. The main contributor to high levels of lead in the air in the studio environment is the lead dust (oxide) that was a main ingredient in traditional glazing cement. When old stained glass windows are disassembled for restoration this lead oxide is released into the air. Our first solution was to have our occupational health consultant fit our employees with respirators then we isolated the disassembly room and added a HEPA air filtration system.

Over the last two decades we have periodically invited the voluntary compliance unit of OSHA to visit our studio to help us comply with these very important health and safety regulations. A number of years ago OSHA intensified their regulations for the air quality in all areas of the workplace to meet safe use levels without the use of respirators. In order to meet this new regulation we had to become very creative with our restoration method. We developed a process where the stained glass windows to be restored are disassembled under water (see photos next page). This literally has prevented all of the lead dust from entering the environment's air and we are pleased to report that we have maintained excellent air quality in this area since implementing this system.

Above: Three views of an old stained glass window in need of restoration. The first step is to compose a photographic record and make a pattern rubbing.

Restoration technicians, JoLynn Tolson (top photo) and Mark Steele (bottom photo) carefully disassemble the windows underwater in our specially designed lead reclamation tank. The process is so clean the technicians do not need to wear respirators.

Now the lead dust goes into the water. However, you cannot simply discard lead contaminated water by letting it go down the drain. The EPA's requires a license to process contaminated wastewater, including the simple act of filtering the water for reuse. Our solution is to store the tainted water in tanks until they are shipped to a licensed toxic wastewater treatment facility. Our restoration facility now has excellent air quality and we are not contributing to the contamination of the environment with toxic wastewater.

We identified another problem area was during the removal of windows from their frame prior to restoration. We developed a process that uses a portable HEPA filter system that picks up lead dust that may fall off of the glazing cement, the lead came or the window sash that may come loose during removal of the stained glass windows.

Traditional formulas for glass paints and stains contain lead oxide. Many modern opaque painting formulas have successfully eliminated the lead content however, no one has come up with a formula to eliminate the lead content in the transparent color palate. Since we could not eliminate the use of lead oxide paints we had to devise a solution to protect our staff in the glass painting area. Initially we tried using portable HEPA filtering systems set up next to the workstations. Unfortunately we could not achieve consistent low lead air levels in the glass painting studio. We brought in professional help to design and install a large 18 foot (5.5 m) high HEPA filtration system with elaborate ductwork built into the artists' glass painting studio to clean the air. We literally had to raise the roof to install this air filter to meet OSHA's air quality regulations.

Lead in the environment is a serious concern. The EPA can and does issue very large fines for the improper disposal of lead. Years ago we would sell our scrap lead to a salvage yard for a few dollars and it was simply placed in a pile in the yard. We now know this is unacceptable. Laws and regulations have changed, fines have increased and over time the amount of lead allowed into the environment has been greatly reduced. Today the lead came manufacturers themselves have set up programs to recapture any scrap lead returning it directly back for recycling. We now ship our old lead in sealed metal barrels directly back to the lead smelter for recycling. Last year we returned almost 14,000 lbs (6300 kg) of lead for recycling. This not only protects our workers and the environment from possible contamination but ensures that Bovard Studio and our clients are responsible environmental citizens.

Butterfly Dreams Take Flight

HOLY TRINITY Roman Catholic Church, Des Moines, Iowa is a simple cinder block structure that was built the 1960's. It has long straight walls and steel framed windows that run horizontally along the upper section of the walls. I met with Father Laurenzo in September 1992 as they were in the planning stages to renovate their worship space. The existing windows were glazed with an unimaginative arrangement of odd colored sheets of stained glass. Father Laurenzo had the vision to incorporate the symbol for Pope John Paul II's trip to Iowa in 1979. This symbol consisted of a butterfly design that used a cross image for the body that expanded out to divide its beautiful wings into the colors of the four seasons.

The Father and I worked up a series of thumbnail sketches for the design. I took these back to the studio to be executed into a rendering by one of our artists. Within days, Father Laurenzo approved one of the designs and the project was started.

We divided and expanded this symbol for the resurrection of Jesus Christ to fit the length of the two 61' x 5-1/2' (18.6 m x 1.7 m) nave windows. The structure of the cross was kept in the center of each window with two of the four seasons displayed in each stained glass window. This installation transformed an awkward aspect of Holy Trinity's worship space into a radiant jewel adding significant meaning for worship.

Center panel detail from the Spring-Summer design

Two photos of the installation: the upper photo shows the full length of the Spring-Summer panel and the lower photo is the Autumn-Winter design.

Below: Thumbnail sketches created by Ron Bovard showing variations on the butterfly theme.

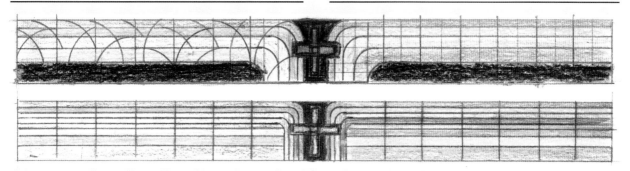

Structural Reinforcing

THE IMPORTANCE OF STRUCTURAL COMPOSITION was discussed in an earlier chapter during the designing process (see page 48). The designer made some calculations and limited the individual sections in the window to 12 square feet (1.2 square meters) or less and has made provisions for all other structural requirements based on the window's design and proportion.

Above & right: These views clearly show how the oversized areas within a window's framework is divided into smaller sections with mullions, muntins, and steel horizontal T-bars.

Mark Steele is installing the massive "Hand of God" window for Maxwell Air Force Base, Montgomery, Alabama.

STRUCTURE AND REINFORCING

Reinforcing

Lead is a very soft metal providing the flexibility that enables the fabricator to easily shape the lead came strips to fit around the curves and bends in the window's design. Unfortunately, the lead alone does not possess sufficient tensile strength to hold any substantial weight within the frame on its own. If a stained glass window were fabricated and installed as one large section, the weight of the upper leaded section would press down upon the lower panels causing them to bow and eventually collapse. You often see this occurring in older leaded glass windows. Imagine a set of children's building blocks stacked up. As long as the blocks are stacked up in a perfectly flat vertical plane, they are stable. Once the stack begins to bow, instability increases exponentially with the increasing degree of deflection (bowing and bulging) and they all come tumbling down. The same is true of leaded glass windows.

To minimize this problem, the window frame is divided into several smaller independent sections (and therefore so is the stained glass window). These frame dividers are called mullions and usually add a decorative pattern to the window framing in addition to ensuring stability for the leaded glass. Any section or opening within the window's frame that is larger than 12 square feet (1.2 square meters) should be further divided with horizontal T-bars (called muntins). These steel or aluminum T-bars are fastened securely to the window's framework. They supplement the mullions to transfer the weight of the upper leaded glass panels to the window frame, rather than entrusting the lower stained glass panels to support the weight of the upper panels.

In addition to the mullions and muntins breaking the window frame into smaller sections, the leaded glass windows also require supplemental reinforcing. The traditional method of supplemental window reinforcing is to install the leaded window sections then affix horizontal steel bars into the sash of the window frame at 1-1/2 to 2 foot (45.7 to 61 cm) intervals. These steel bars would be on the inside of the stained glass and would be attached to the leaded panel using copper wires that are soldered to the lead came and wrapped around the steel reinforcing bar.

A contemporary method of supplemental reinforcing is to use galvanized flat steel bar that is 1/8" thick x 1/2" wide (3 mm x 1.3 cm) and is cut slightly longer than the window is wide. This flat bar is set perpendicular (90°) to the glass surface and laid horizontally across the width of panel. The bar is soldered directly to the lead came wherever it contacts a solder joint. To achieve maximum stability it is essential that the ends of the reinforcing bar be firmly attached to the window frame on installation.

A window showing areas of bowing and bulging at the bottom from the weight of the sections above.

Mark Steele soldering steel reinforcing bars to a stained glass panel at the Maxwell Air Force Base Chapel. Eighteen inches (46 cm) is the typical spacing for reinforcing bars. Artistic considerations as well as structural requirements may affect the final placement of the reinforcing bars.

PROTECTIVE EXTERIOR COVERING

Protective Covering

STAINED GLASS WINDOWS in a church or temple are intended to artistically illuminate, beautify and spiritually uplift the interior space while also forming an integral component of the architectural texture of the building's exterior. Protective glazing is often added to the windows on the exterior of a building with the intention of protecting the stained glass from vandalism and storm damage and to add some measure of insulation for energy conservation. The problem is this protective glazing can drastically reduce or even eliminate the visibility of significant architectural features of a building's exterior facade, such as the intricate traceries of a compound window frame and the leaded panes of the stained glass windows.

Let's examine the issue of insulating value for energy conservation. Churches that are heated intermittently, that is heated occasionally for services then allowed to cool back, will not experience a significant saving in heating expenses. This conclusion was reached in a 1996 study of 'Protective Glazing' that was commissioned by the National Center for Technology and Training (conducted by Inspired Partnerships Inc. Chicago, Illinois). This study examined data from 160 churches in the Chicago area and found that the energy saving benefit derived from the installation of exterior glazing was minimal for intermittently heated buildings. The report is titled 'Protective Glazing Study' and is available on the NCPTT website: http://www.ncptt.nps.gov/

However this study did not go so far as to say that exterior glazing did not improve the quality of the heat inside the building. It cannot be disputed that cold air will draft through and around a stained glass window in addition to an increase in humidity from condensation and leaks as a result of wind driven rain; all these are inherent in any single glazed system. Heating and cooling cycles promote expansion and contraction of the stained glass window and this movement will loosen the glazing cement that is packed between the flanges of the lead came and the stained glass, eventually producing leakage (see cementing page 54). The traditional method to handle this condensation and leakage was to install collection pans at the bottom of the stained glass windows. Medieval gothic cathedrals with stone frames had these water collection troughs carved directly into the stone sash. Some frames even had these water collection gutters slope in from both sides to the middle with a weep hole cut through the frame to channel the collected water to the exterior of the building, in some cases out through a gargoyle's mouth.

An exterior covering reduces air infiltration, improves the security of the building and reduces the likelihood of vandal or storm damage to the window.

A modern window with exterior glass in an aluminum frame that has built in ventilation.

A properly designed and installed exterior glazing system will create an effective barrier to prevent cold air drafts and rain leakage. In addition it will reduce the consequence of vandalism and storm damage. It is imperative to specify a protective glazing system that is a proven and effective barrier to ensure the precious stained glass heritage is preserved for future generations.

Unfortunately follow up studies, conducted to measure the effectiveness of protective glazing installed in the US, indicate that these windows have suffered more damage to the stained glass and their frames from improperly designed protective glazing systems than from damage caused by storms, fires and vandalism combined. How could this happen? The primary cause is the condensation that naturally forms on the interior side of the exterior glazing. In a single glazed system the stained window is the exterior glazing and this condensation moisture is collected at the bottom of the window and allowed to evaporate into the interior of the building (see previous paragraph). However, in an unvented double glazed system, as is the case with a stained glass window and a protective glazing, the condensation moisture is trapped within the closed airspace. A continuously damp space such as this, is conducive to the growth of microorganisms that secrete organic acids that attack the stained glass, oxidize the lead and metal frames and rot wooden frames.

Additionally this unvented space is also a serious heat trap. The 'Protective Glazing' study (mentioned in the 2nd paragraph on page 60) found air temperatures of up to 165°F (74°C) trapped in the air space, exaggerating the expansion and contraction cycle. It is widely accepted that expansion and contraction cycles deteriorate most building materials, including stained glass windows, causing reinforcing systems to fail, premature metal fatigue and deterioration of both the frame and the lead in a stained glass window. The super heated air also creates pressure on the stained glass window and protective glazing, contributing to the deflection of the stained glass window. From our observations while restoring stained glass windows with these types of problems, the less the space between the stained glass window and the unvented protective covering, the more severe the damage becomes - the greater the space, the less severe the damage. A quick visual inspection will give clear evidence if a moisture problem exists. From the outside of the building look at the surface of the lead behind the protective covering, if you detect a white powder you have found 'lead oxide' (the equivalent of rust on steel) and this window may have a problem (see photo above right). If the window frames are wood, check for rot; if steel, check for rust; if stone, check for spalling. From the interior, check the stained glass window for sagging, bulging and cracks in the stained glass panes and the glass pulling out of the flanges of the lead came in these areas. These indicators are evidence that the stained glass windows are in need of expert care.

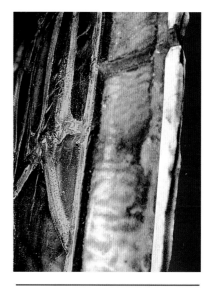

This window has a white "lead oxide" powder (the equivalent of rust on steel) on the surface of the lead indicating it had a problem with moisture build-up between the protective covering and the stained glass window.

Vents were drilled (note upper section) for this installation.

Venting produced by drilling holes in the exterior glazing that is covered using screened vent plugs with a rain guard feature.

A new stained glass window showing the ventilation system built into an aluminum frame, private chapel, Wichita, Kansas.

So what can be done? The solution, to eliminate both the moisture and heat build up in the closed space between stained glass window and a protective glazing is actually quite simple – adequate ventilation! One square inch (6.5 SqCm) of ventilation at the top and another one at the bottom of the stained glass window is the minimum ventilation recommended for 16 SqFt (1.5 SqM) of stained glass within a 'closed' double glazed system. If the protective covering is being placed over previously installed stained glass windows the venting is produced by drilling holes in the exterior glazing that are covered using screened vent plugs with a rain guard feature. When a new stained glass window is being created for a preinstalled frame that already has exterior glazing (either single or insulated units) the venting is allocated to the interior side, as part of the stained glass framing, allowing the equivalent of a minimum of one square inch (6.5 SqCm) at the top and bottom per 16 SqFt (1.5 SqM) of stained glass.

Bovard Studio is resolute to the essential necessity for venting to maintain and preserve stained glass that we dedicated our resources to find the best possible solution. Our engineers and experienced field staff researched and proposed several venting solutions before settling on a method that could be built directly into the frame creating a seamless installation that provided more than enough ventilation while preventing water and insect infiltration. We refined and tested our designs and finally arrived at our Precision Flow® ventilation system. We received our official Patent Pending status in November 2003 and are hoping to receive our final patent approvals at any time.

Our Precision Flow® ventilation system can be retro-fitted into in a frame where the exterior glazing is pre-existing (the vents are placed on the interior side of the installation) or it can be built into a frame to hold the exterior glazing (whether in a single glazed or insulated unit system). We have a Precision Flow® ventilation solution for all types of frame applications including, single glazed interior installations, protective exterior glazing (single and double glazed), thermal barrier aluminum frames and traditional wood frames.

Specifications for the Precision Flow® ventilation system is a minimum of one SqIn (6.5 SqCm) of ventilation (at both the bottom and top of the unit) per 16 SqFt (1.5 SqM) of stained glass. The venting ports are precisely positioned to promote optimum airflow and an easy escape for the heat and condensation. Exterior venting solutions have a water shield to prevent water from wind driven rain from entering into the system. In addition, perforated aluminum screens are placed flush with the exterior surface area to prevent insects from entering or nesting in or around the vents, blocking the air flow and cause the ventilation system to fail.

Adequate ventilation is essential but it is only one consideration for a properly designed and installed exterior glazing system. The other consideration is the choice of glazing material. There are several types of materials available for protective glazing systems for stained glass windows, they are: standard float glass, laminated glass, tempered glass, laminated-tempered glass, polycarbonate (Lexan™), acrylic (Plexiglass™), and extended life polycarbonate (polycarbonate with a coating of acrylic).

THERE ARE PROS AND CONS FOR EACH OF THESE CATEGORIES:

• Standard float glass maintains a clear, colorless appearance, is resistant to scratching and is less expensive than any of the other material choices. Its disadvantage is its relative lack of strength and when broken the shards become a safety hazard, especially during windstorms or earthquakes.

• Laminated glass has the same properties as standard float glass with one important distinction; it holds together when broken and will continue to protect the window from most hurled projectiles. This is an invaluable safety feature in severe storm and earthquake zones.

• Tempered glass maintains all of the attributes of float glass with the added benefit of having 10 times more resistance to breakage from impact. If tempered glass does break it shatters into countless small shards, making it unusable in locations with hurricane and severe weather codes. The broken bits of glass become high velocity projectiles that can be fatal in fierce winds.

• Laminated-Tempered glass combines all of the clarity and beauty of float glass with the strength of tempered glass and the safety of laminated glass. The only drawback is it is expensive.

• Plastic polycarbonate (Lexan™) is virtually shatter proof. Unfortunately it tends to yellow when exposed to ultraviolet (sun) light and is susceptible to hazing from wind blown particulates. Polycarbonate expands as the outside temperature rises, causing it to flex during these expansion cycles creating an unattractive glare as light reflects off of the concave or convex surfaces. This effect can be minimized by using the more rigid 1/4" (6 mm) thick material and compensated for in the framing system.

• Acrylic (Plexiglas™) is hard and somewhat brittle and that means it is shatter resistant (but can break). It does block most of the UV light that causes the yellowing in polycarbonate however it will haze from wind blown particulates. Acrylic has a similar coefficient of expansion to that of polycarbonate and the same precautions due to flexing apply.

• Acrylic coated polycarbonate (Extended Life Lexan - XL10™) is a product that has been developed combining these 2 materials. The acrylic coating is harder, providing more resistance to scratching, and it protects the polycarbonate from ultraviolet (sun) light to reduce yellowing. The polycarbonate is virtually shatter proof providing a greater level of security.

Don Berg is working on a new mahogany wood frame being fabricated in our shop. It will have a Precision Flow® ventilation system built directly into the frame. Notice the vent hole at lower right in the photo.

Tempered glass (1/4" - 6 mm) protective glazing system with ventilation built into a new wood frame for St. Paul's Episcopal Church, Missouri.

LOW-E COATED FLOAT GLASS

When standard float glass is selected as the exterior glazing it's important to be aware of a special type of glass called 'Low-E' that is fast becoming a popular choice for many building installations. Low-emittance (a.k.a. Low-E) glass is coated with microscopic layers of anti-reflective metal or metallic oxide designed to suppress the radiative transfer of heat. Various types of Low-E coatings have been developed that allow for high solar gain, moderate solar gain, or low solar gain. One variation of this glass, used in colder climates, has the dual effect of admitting heat (high solar gain) through the glass while at the same time reducing heat loss from inside the building. Another type, (low solar gain) is used in warmer climates and reacts in the reverse manner, to deflect heat away from the window glass on the exterior.

Low-E coated glass has promising possibilities to enhance heating and cooling efficiencies, however if the wrong Low-E type glass is used as an exterior glazing for stained glass windows it can cause significant problems. The Low-E coating functions to either block the solar energy transfer or allow it to pass through, depending on the specific characteristics of the coating type.

A 'high solar gain' Low-E glazing system allows the solar energy to pass through the Low-E window glass while suppressing the heat from passing back out through the glass. If a stained glass window is installed on the interior side, the heat is blocked from entering the building by the stained glass window. This heat is then trapped between the stained glass window and the Low-E glass (that prevents transfer back out) thereby amplifying the heat build up.

The 'low solar gain' type of Low-E coating reflects a significant quantity of solar energy. This effectively reduces the amount of heat that enters through the exterior glass that could be trapped between the stained glass window and protective glazing. However any heat that does enter the space, either from the inside or outside, has resistance escaping back out through the Low-E window glass and would be trapped in a non-vented system.

There are several other variations in coating types. One type, called 'sputter coating' allows a greater amount of heat transfer as the sun becomes lower on the horizon, as typically occurs during the winter months. This is seen as an advantage when the consideration is for heating the interior of the building, but as you might imagine this special function would increase the heat build up if a stained glass window were installed on the inside, thereby blocking the heat transfer.

This acrylic coated polycarbonate exterior glazing was retrofitted to this older window frame. It was vented by drilling holes at both the top and bottom. These holes were then fitted with vent plugs that are covered with screen and have a rain guard feature.

Typically, the most immediate failure is in the Low-E glass itself. This glass can get very hot due to its exposure to the solar energy, however the portion of the Low-E glass that is set into the sash is not exposed to this heat gain and stays cooler. When this difference in temperature is exaggerated by the heat buildup in an unventilated space it can create enough stress to crack the Low-E glass pane. We have seen specific examples of damage when a combination of Low-E glass and stained glass windows are installed in non-vented protective glazing systems. The Low-E glass cracked and the new stained glass windows severely buckled within a short period of time.

We have had meaningful discussions with several Low-E glass manufacturers concerning the efficacy of using this treated glass in combination with stained glass. All of the experts agree that adequate ventilation is required between Low-E glass and stained glass windows (as is true with stained glass windows and any exterior glazing system).

We have installed stained glass windows on the inside of Low-E glass exterior glazing systems using the calculation of 1 square inch per 16 square feet at the top and bottom of the unit, the same ventilation allowance that we use for standard protective glazing systems. Every job that we have installed with this allowance has been successful (to date). The consequence of installing stained glass windows behind Low-E glass is anecdotal at best. Clear-cut recommendations cannot be determined until systematic studies have been conducted on the various Low-E coatings in installations with stained glass windows.

Above: An engineered protective glazing installation for First United Methodist Church in Iowa City, Iowa. The elaborate glazing process uses aluminum framing material that is custom bent to match the rose window's mullion tracery. The center circle and each petal on the rose design has a new aluminum frame secured to the top of the original wooden frame. Then each section is fitted with laminated glass (double glass with a plastic core). The venting for this installation was accomplished by creating hidden portals strategically located in the bent metal frame.

PROTECTIVE GLAZING CONCLUSIONS

Protective glazing systems should be designed to minimize the aesthetic impact on the stained glass window and on the architectural features of the building. In addition it is essential to build in adequate ventilation to ensure the preservation of our nation's precious stained glass heritage for future generations.

Essential Elements

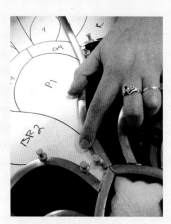

The photograph shows a window being leaded up using extruded "lead alloy" came.

Nick Davis is placing steel reinforcing bars on this window section which will hold the stained glass panel in a flat plane.

A CORRECTLY DESIGNED and fabricated leaded glass window has several elements that are essential.

A professionally designed, structurally fabricated, and properly reinforced leaded glass window will require little or no maintenance for the first 60 to 70 years of its existence. In order for a stained glass window to meet this standard, the following factors must be present:

• The framework of a large window must be subdivided with mullions to create smaller sections. These mullions usually add a decorative pattern to the window framing in addition to ensuring stability for the leaded glass.

• Individual leaded glass panel sections should be 12 square feet (1.2 square meters) or less. Any section or opening within the window's frame that is larger than 12 square feet (1.2 square meters), should be further divided with horizontal T-bars (called muntins). These steel or aluminum T-bars are fastened securely to the window's framework. They supplement the mullions, to transfer the weight of the upper leaded glass panels to the window frame, rather than entrusting the lower stained glass panels to support the weight of the upper panels.

• Leaded glass designs that have a high number of smaller pieces, or designs that feature concentric geometric patterns, should be smaller than 12 square feet (1.2 square meters) per individual section.

• Leaded glass windows must be fabricated with lead came that has sufficient tensile strength. For this reason it is crucial to use a lead came manufactured by the extrusion process using a lead alloy that contains antimony, silver, copper, or tin. Milled came made from pure lead (without alloy additives) is too soft and will not hold up for as long, even under normal conditions.

• The leaded glass windows must be properly sealed with a commercial cementing compound or putty that is pressed under the flanges of the lead came. Once the cement has set, it will make the panel more rigid and weather tight.

• In addition to a well engineered matrix of mullions and muntins, leaded panels must have a supplemental reinforcing system. Steel re-bars must be securely soldered or wire tied to the lead came and attached to the window frame. The proper function of a reinforcing bar is to hold the stained glass in a flat plane; it is not to hold the stained glass up. Once the stained glass begins to sag or bulge out of a flat plane it becomes weak and will tend to bulge more and more until the lateral pressure on the glass causes it to break. The smaller the stained glass component parts, the closer the steel reinforcing bars need to be, on average every 18 inches (45.7cm) is sufficient spacing. Of course, artistic design requirements may also affect the placement of the reinforcing bars. Be warned, without a properly designed reinforcing system, the stained glass window will not withstand the test of time. For more information please refer to Chapter 12 - Structure and Reinforcing on page 58.

• If an exterior protective covering is installed it must be properly vented to allow the moisture that collects in the space between the stained glass window and protective covering to dry out between condensation cycles. For more information please refer to Chapter 13 – Protective Exterior Covering on page 60.

Right: Steel reinforcing bars are placed approximately every 18 inches (45.7cm) however, artistic design requirements may also affect the placement of the reinforcing bars. Here we see Mark Steele bending the rebar to follow along a gentle curve in the windows lead design.

Above & Right: A 17' (5.2 m) Rose Window for Christ The King Catholic Church, Ann Arbor, Michigan. This design was inspired by a stained glass window in St. Peter's Cathedral, Rome, Italy.

Plum Street Temple

Plum Street Temple in Cincinnati, Ohio, one of the first Reform synagogues in the U.S., was opened to the public on August 23, 1866.

After 134 years, the stained glass windows were in need of a complete restoration.

"THE WISE and republican laws of this Country are based upon universal toleration giving to every citizen and sojourner the right to worship according to the dictates of his conscience." These words were written in 1840 at the birth of the congregation B'nai Yeshurun at the old Workum House on Third Street between Sycamore and Broadway in Cincinnati, Ohio; forming a new fundamental principle as the basis of their constitution.

"A religious Jew can also be a citizen of a free country, a member of society, a reasoner of modern thought," words of Isaac Mayer Wise who became the Rabbi of the B'nai Yeshurum congregation in 1854. Wise was a supporter of the Reform movement that wanted to give Judaism a distinctly American look. Rabbi Wise soon made Cincinnati a center of Reform Judaism in the United States as he became a founder of Hebrew Union College in Cincinnati as well as the Union of American Hebrew Congregations. To this day Plum Street Temple hosts ordination services for the Cincinnati Campus of the Hebrew Union College, which ordains all Reform rabbis in the United States.

On August 23, 1866 the Plum Street Temple in Cincinnati, Ohio, one of the first Reform synagogues in the U.S., was opened to the public as the new home of the congregation B'nai Yeshurum. The American architect, James Keys Wilson, designed the Plum Street Temple in the Moorish style that was equated with Jewish aesthetic and spiritual values that coincided with the flowering of Judaic culture under the Moslem caliphate in Spain during the Middle Ages.

The unique Plum Street Temple, now designated a National Historic Landmark, is preeminent among Reform Synagogues in America.

By August 2000, after 134 years, the stained glass windows were in need of a complete restoration as the stained glass windows' lead matrix had succumbed to metal fatigue. Over the next few months Bovard Studio restored all 71 stained glass windows in Plum Street Temple's stained glass heritage, preserving these original historic stained glass windows for future generations.

See photo on opposite page top left for a spectacular view of the restored interior of this great temple.

Plum Street Temple (see page 68) is now designated a National Historic Landmark. Bovard Studio restored all 71 stained glass windows, thereby preserving these unique historic windows for future generations.

A new memorial window for The Veterans Administration Hospital in Knoxville, Iowa.

A new 'Christ in Gethsemane' window made for the Little Rock Missionary Baptist Church, Detroit, Michigan.

An English Country Chapel

BAKER UNIVERSITY CHAPEL, BALDWIN, KANSAS

An historic English chapel was moved stone by stone from its rural setting in England to the campus of Baker University in Baldwin, Kansas. Now perfectly restored, this beautiful chapel looks as if it had been there from the very beginning. A refined English style garden blends the rear of the Chapel into the surrounding Kansas landscape.

The Chapel windows are exquisite examples of English traditional stained glass design. The greatest responsibility in this restoration project was to find a suitable replacement glass and to recreate the painted details for the broken and missing components damaged in handling and transport from England to Kansas. The client challenged our artists to produce replacement pieces that were indistinguishable from the original.

We completed the restoration and installed the windows back into the Chapel's beautifully carved stone frames. We stood back to carefully scrutinize the windows and searched in vain as even our trained eyes could not differentiate the original glass from the replaced pieces of hand-painted glass.

At the Chapel's rededication ceremony, dignitaries and special guests assembled for the occasion. The sanctuary was animated in anticipation of the arrival of the special guest speaker. This individual had spent many Sundays of her youth here, as her father was the Pastor for the congregation at this rural English chapel. As the appointed time arrived, a warm reception was offered to the former Prime Minister of England, the honorable Margaret Thatcher.

Exterior view of the restored windows installed back into the Chapel's beautifully carved stone window frames. Below right: A refined English style garden landscapes the backyard of the Chapel.

The sanctuary was animated in anticipation of the arrival of the special guest speaker. This individual had spent many Sundays of her youth here, as her father was the Pastor for the congregation at this rural English chapel.

Baker Chapel

This historic English chapel was moved from its rural setting in England to the campus of Baker University. The chancel windows above were restored by Bovard Studio and are exquisite examples of traditional English design.

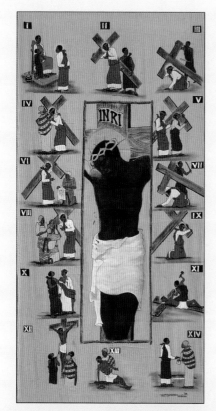

A Tapestry Of Inspirations

THE WINDOW COMMITTEE at St. Benedict the Moor Roman Catholic Church was searching for a studio to design and fabricate 14 stained glass windows for their new sanctuary. They wanted the design to reflect the faith and legacy of this principally African American community in Dayton, Ohio. The church had a tapestry that was made by Father Francis Tandoh depicting the 14 Stations of the Cross in an African design style. The window committee challenged us to interpret the 14 scenes on this tapestry into 14 stained glass windows.

Some of our design staff (myself included) had concerns about how satisfactorily these tapestry images would translate into stained glass windows. As it turned out, our doubts were unfounded. These windows were brilliant and spectacular thanks to the talent and skill of our design team and stained glass artists.

Left: A tapestry made by Father Francis Tandoh, depicting the 14 Stations of the Cross, was used by Bovard's design staff as the inspiration for the stained glass windows. The scenes below represent the 5th, 10th and 12th Stations of the Cross and the panels on page 73 represent the 1st, 6th and 8th Stations.

Father Tandoh's original 'Stations of the Cross' artwork (shown on opposite page at the upper left) came from his heart and soul. The stained glass panels based on his art communicate a fresh and heartfelt interpretation of the passion of Christ, infused with a unique cultural flavor.

Below: Details from Father Francis Tandoh's tapestry is shown above the stained glass panel that was created from the tapestry.

Note: The window shown at top left on page 121 was fabricated and installed in this same church.

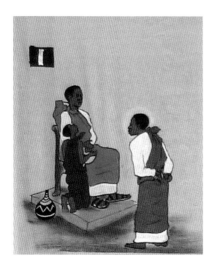

19

Category 4 Hurricane Iniki

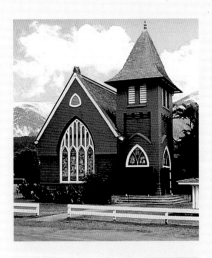

Waioli Hui'ia Church has been designated a National Historic Landmark. It is located in Hanalei, Kaua'i, Hawaii.

WAIOLI HUI'IA CHURCH sits at the old Mission founded in 1834 on Kauai, in the heart of Hanalei. On September 11, 1992 at 3:30 p.m. HST, hurricane Iniki made landfall on the southern coast of Kauai, with maximum sustained winds of 140 mph and gusts even higher, making Iniki a Category 4 hurricane on the Saffir-Simpson scale. Hurricane Iniki was a big one by any standards. The Waioli Hui'ia Church was literally lifted off if its foundation, causing extensive damage to the building's structure and smashing the Church's precious stained glass heritage. The proud church had been designated a National Historic Landmark but it is much more than a landmark to the regional community of Hanalei and to all citizens of Hawaii.

The Queen of Kauai, Deborah Kapule was an early Christian convert and helped establish the Mission in the 1830's on land provided by Governor Kaikioewa of Kauai. The historic Mission House was built in 1837 and the adjoining Mission Hall was finished in 1843, resplendent with its tower belfry and requisite mission bell. The current church building was constructed on this site in 1912 and the original Mission

Figurative, abstract, traditional, minimal, modern, ornate, bright contrasting colors, or with subtle shades. Whether housed in a great cathedral or a humble country church, stained glass at its best should reflect the soul of the congregation, the spirit of God manifest on Earth. - R. B.

House and Mission Hall were fully restored that same year. The church has enjoyed an uninterrupted succession of services since 1834, first as a Congregational Church and since 1957 as a United Church of Christ.

In the aftermath of hurricane Iniki the restoration committee appointed Alfonso J. Garza, of Designare Architects in Honolulu, as the restoration architect and Callahan Construction of Hanalei, Hawaii, was awarded the general contract. They conducted a national search for a qualified stained glass studio to restore the heavily damaged windows and recreate the destroyed stained glass. Their search eventually brought them to our studio and after many discussions and consultations we were awarded the contract. It struck me that the geographic contrasts could not be greater. Bovard Studio, surrounded by the cornfields and big blue sky of Iowa, and the Waioli Hui'ia Church sitting at the base of a volcano on one of the most beautiful islands in the world. We were two disparate partners with one noble and unified objective.

In November of 1993 our restoration team arrived at the Waioli Hui'ia Church to extract the windows. The process begins by first assessing the damage and then photographically recording the current condition of windows, it is important to have accurate site records that often prove invaluable during the restoration. The windows were carefully removed and all previously recovered bits and pieces were located before everything was crated for shipment to our studio back in Iowa.

Four sets of double lancet stained glass windows had to be recreated. Matching historic opalescent stained glass is exponentially more difficult than matching paint color or dye lots. In glass, we not only have to match a unique combination of color mix, but we must match the density and the unique refractory qualities of the light as it passes through the glass.

We put out a call to our trusted suppliers and opalescent glass manufacturers to search their hoard of old glass for suitable matches. To our delight, they successfully located a match for all the replacement glass we needed, except one. The main background glass for all of the Waioli Hui'ia Church's stained glass windows was a green, amber and white opalescent that was not currently available. We looked at dozens of color samples from current production glass and decided to ask Youghiogheny Opalescent Glass Company to recreate a glass to match the original. Their skilled colorists were able to achieve a nearly perfect match. However since the density, color and consistency of opalescent glass actually changes during the course of batch production, it was the glass three-fourths of the way through the batch that was selected as the best match.

The restored windows were shipped 4,000 miles back to Kauai and meticulously reinstalled into the rebuilt Waioli Hui'ai Church in time for the Church's dedication ceremonies in April of 1994. We were thrilled with the results as was the restoration architect and the church's congregation. We have been told that even the most discerning visitor is amazed to learn the stained glass windows have undergone extensive restoration.

Cleaning & Maintenance

THE GOOD NEWS IS stained glass windows do not show dirt and grime as readily as a clear glass window does. However, there is a course of action that you can take to keep your new windows looking immaculate or to bring back the luster to an older installation.

The primary cleaning for a stained glass window is to simply dust the inside surface occasionally with a soft brush. When a more meticulous cleaning is required, it is important to be conscientious of any painted areas on the window. Painted stained glass and particularly areas with enamel paint (opaque colors) are especially sensitive to acids, which means a vinegar and water solution could easily damage these areas. Be sure to test all painted areas with your cleaning solution prior to any thorough cleaning and avoid any areas in doubt. If your testing finds the painted areas to be stable, they may be safely cleaned along with the non-painted areas of the window.

Stained glass windows should be washed using a soft cotton cloth and a pH neutral cleaning solution mixed with distilled water.

Detail, St. Cecilia window.

St. Cecilia window for the St. Cecilia Church in Ames, Iowa.

Stained glass windows should be washed using a soft cotton cloth and a pH neutral cleaning solution mixed with distilled water. An excellent product is Triton X-100, a professional quality, non-ionic detergent (made by City Chemical Company of NY). However, most horse shampoos (available from any equine tack shop) are a safe and very effective alternative for cleaning stained glass windows. Since horse skin is more sensitive than human skin, horse shampoos are formulated to be pH neutral. Some cleaning compounds to be avoided are any that contain acid bases such as vinegar and ammonia and never use abrasives, scouring powders or steel wool scrubbers.

If your test cleaning indicates that the painted areas are unstable, especially if you found loose or flaking areas, it is better to leave the dirt on the stained glass rather than chance further damage to the window. Unstable paint could be the consequence of age, or may indicate the original artist used an improper paint formula or incorrect kiln firing procedure. Some historic stained glass windows were actually "cold painted" using standard air-dry paints that can easily be scraped or washed off the glass. When the window reaches the point of requiring a complete restoration, a qualified stained glass restoration company will address the problem of the unstable glass paint.

A new hand-painted stained glass window of Christ blessing the children made for St. Edward The Confessor Roman Catholic Church in New Fairfield, Connecticut.

Installation of a restored Tiffany window including laminated glass protective covering. See Chapter 13, page 60 for more information on exterior protective coverings.

In addition to an occasional cleaning, the steel reinforcing system needs to be checked periodically to ensure it remains attached to the window's lead matrix. As leaded glass windows age, normal expansion and contraction may break the copper tie wires away from the round steel reinforcing bars. Or, if the more modern flat steel reinforcing bars are used, the solder joints connecting them to the lead matrix of your stained glass windows can break loose. The reinforcing bars need to be reattached to the lead matrix by repairing the wires or solder joints. This is a job for a professional stained glass restoration company. Windows assembled with dividing steel T-bars need to be inspected periodically for rust on the steel. If found, the corrosion must be removed and the surface repainted.

Finally, windows set into their frames with glaziers putty should have any loose or missing putty replaced on a regular basis. To maintain a strong physical integrity, a stained glass window depends on a solid setting and tight installation.

Time and money spent on preventative maintenance will save money in the end as it prolongs the life of your stained glass and delays the time until costly restoration will be required. Few products made today are expected to last for centuries. Stained glass windows have a long life expectancy and a good maintenance program will preserve your stained glass heritage for centuries.

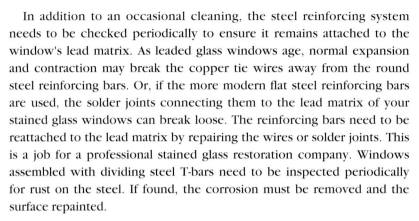

Above and Right: This series of four historic windows was created by the famous stained glass artist Frederick Lamb. They were releaded and restored by Bovard Studio for The First Presbyterian Church, Davenport, Iowa.

Faceted Glass

Faceted Tiles Of Glass

DALLE DE VERRE (French for "tiles of glass") also called faceted glass windows, use one inch (2.5 cm) thick slabs of glass, cut into the desired shapes then selectively faceted on the interior edges to enhance the refraction of light. The design process for a dalle de verre window is similar to that of a leaded glass window. However, the fabrication process is entirely different. The cut and faceted pieces of glass are arranged on a casting table in a mold according to the pattern design. Then an epoxy resin is poured between each piece to create the structural matrix. Finally, the resin is covered with a layer of colored granules. We strongly recommend the use of black or very dark colored granules unless a very specific effect is desired. The black colored matrix will result in a uniform presentation on the exterior of the building, much like a solid sheet of glass. A light colored matrix seems to produce an unsettling disorder that often conflicts with the architecture of the building.

Above: Dalle de verre or faceted glass windows are fabricated using one inch (2.5 cm) thick slabs of glass. An epoxy resin is poured between each glass piece to create the structural matrix, which shows as black lines in the photograph.

Faceted glass window installation, for Branson Hills Assembly of God, Branson, Missouri.

FACETED GLASS (DALLE DE VERRE) WINDOWS

Faceted Glass

While a protective covering is not required for faceted glass, many architects specify a bronze or tinted sheet of exterior glazing to minimize the impact of the faceted window's resin matrix on the design of their building. In faceted glass windows, the negative space (the matrix) is even more notable than in the design of a leaded glass window, and its impact on the finished artwork is much more pronounced.

Above: Full scale layout pattern for a faceted glass window; the area that will be filled with epoxy are indicated with heavy black lines.

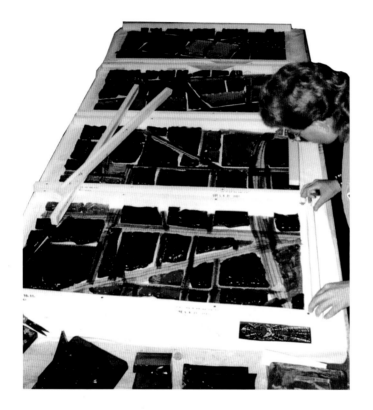

Above left: A faceted glass fabricator lays the dalles and positions the edge blocks to create the mold, prior to "investing" or pouring the epoxy compound between the glass pieces.

An elaborate proposal rendering for a series of faceted glass panels with a contemporary background and minimal emblematic representation.

CARE AND MAINTENANCE

Properly formulated and fabricated faceted glass windows, made with an epoxy matrix, should require no maintenance other than repairing loose glaziers putty or construction sealant around the perimeter of the panels where they are set into the frame.

However, older faceted glass windows fabricated with a portland cement matrix may require extensive repairs and restoration over time. A professional stained glass restoration company should be consulted for problems on this type of window.

This detail close up shows the typical chipped edges on the faceted glass components created using a special hammer and anvil tool. These chips will refract and reflect the light making the window glimmer in the sunlight.

Above: A Computer aided rendition for a faceted glass window with a contemporary design. Notice the creative use of rectangles as a background grid.

Above: A contemporary minimalist interpretation of the symbol for baptism.

St. Peter's Church In Ruins

SAN FRANCISCO'S MISSION DISTRICT was a neighborhood of Irish immigrants. On July 4, 1886, they celebrated our nation's birthday by dedicating the just completed St. Peter's Church. As you enter through the narthex into the nave your attention is pulled upward by the elaborate grisaille style stained glass windows and then beyond to the highest arch of the Trompe L'Oiel painted ceiling where a message from the prophet Isaiah is written: "I have loved, oh Lord, the beauty of thy house and the place where thy glory dwelleth".

Tragedy stuck their city in 1906 with the great San Francisco earthquake and fire. Somehow, St. Peter's, seemingly under divine protection, was one of only five churches left standing. Then on January 17, 1997, a votive candle flickering on the Sacred Heart shrine flared up setting fire to the sanctuary. Father, having a late dinner looked up to see the whole church engulfed in flames. San Francisco's heroic fire fighters arrived and had no choice but to vent the church by smashing St. Peter's stained glass heritage, to extinguish the flames; but St. Peter's lay in ruins. Most of St. Peter's precious historic stained glass windows were broken and blown out. Shards of glass dangled from what was left of the lead matrix. Standing in the nave you could see blue sky where the incredible Trompe L'Oiel painted ceiling had been just a few hours ago.

St. Peter's gloriously ornate interior is unexpected as the relatively plain exterior fits perfectly into San Francisco's historic Mission District.

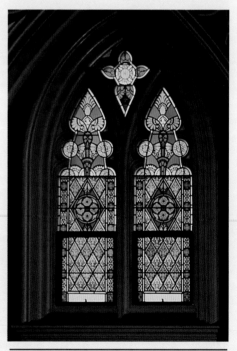

We were able to match both the stained glass and the painting that was on every piece of glass in the windows of St. Peter's church.

The Mission District suddenly felt empty and devoid of vitality the morning after the fire. But St. Peter's (now a 97% Latino parish) like San Francisco herself (after the earthquake and fire of 1906), soon rose from the flames more like the sparkling new church of 1886, than like the elderly matron that had been damaged by fire.

Of St. Peter's 46 stained glass windows, we replicated 38 that were too damaged to be restored. These windows were in the Grisaille style, some with beautiful medallions of saints. There were plenty of shards and panes of glass available to match. We were able to accurately match both the stained glass itself and the glass painting that was on every piece of stained glass in the windows of St. Peter's. Our wood shop made and our craftspeople installed new window frames with hand carved elements in the tracery out of long lasting and stable plantation grown Honduras mahogany for all 46 stained glass windows. We set the new window frames and stained glass windows with laminated tempered glass exterior glazing to meet San Francisco's current earthquake codes.

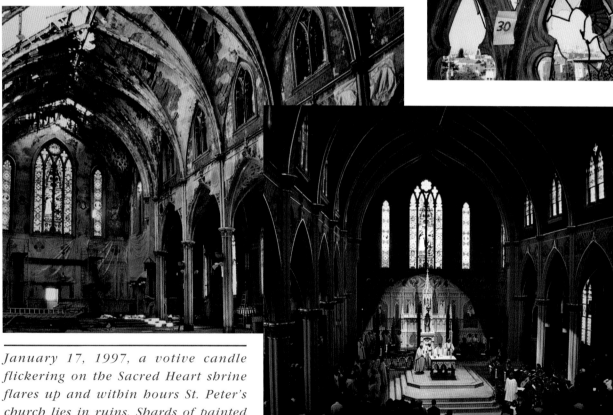

January 17, 1997, a votive candle flickering on the Sacred Heart shrine flares up and within hours St. Peter's church lies in ruins. Shards of painted glass dangle from what is left of the lead matrix. Standing in the nave you can see blue sky where the incredible Trompe L'Oiel painted ceiling once shone.

June 30, 2000; San Francisco worshippers gather to celebrate the rededication of the fully restored St. Peter's church.

VERSION#4
CONCEPT RENDERING FOR
COMPOUND GOTHIC WINDOW#4 (42" X 130")
FIRST CONGREGATIONAL CHURCH, KENOSHA, WI
© 2003 BOVARD STUDIO INC. ALL RIGHTS RESERVED
19/12/03

Our proposal rendering for the 'Angels' window, size, 42" x 130" (1.07 x 3.3 m).

Our Challenge

FIRST CONGREGATIONAL CHURCH of Kenosha, Wisconsin already had two original Tiffany windows. What they were looking for was a new stained glass window created in the 'Tiffany' style, to be installed in the same nave as their originals. So our challenge was to design and create a new window that would hold up, both in design and execution, next to two significant quality original windows by Louis Tiffany and Company (see photos on page 85).

Our designers carefully studied the Tiffany windows and took our style clues for the background and figures from the existing work. We designed a stained glass window with two angels that would stand guard over First Congregational Church, with a laurel wreath of victory (a symbol of having achieved salvation) surrounding the music of the heavenly host. We submitted our proposal renderings and the church selected and approved our 'Angels' design concept.

We consider ourselves very fortunate to have had the opportunity to restore many Tiffany windows over the years. We know that one of the most magical aspects of a Tiffany window is the quality of the glass that is often layered from three to seven plates of stained glass thick. We identified several areas in the two original Tiffany windows that have four to five plates thick. We selected the stained glass for our new window from our own large collection of art glass; we have multiple glass textures and hundreds of colors many of them manufactured by the same companies that supplied Tiffany Studios over 100 years ago. We had a good supply of drapery glass that we used for the angel's robes. This specialty glass, developed by Tiffany and Company has an undulation and wavy surface to simulate the texture of draped fabric (see detail photos on page 86). Drapery glass is made by ladling molten glass onto a graphite table grasping and pulling the glass with tongs while still hot and in a semi-molten state until it has been manipulated into fabric-like draped folds. The thickness of this glass varies from 1/8" to 1-1/2" (3.2 mm to 38 mm) thick. In the finished

These two authentic Louis Tiffany and Company windows are installed in the nave of First Congregational Church of Kenosha, Wisconsin. The quality and luminance of the glass is both magical and exquisite.

First Congregational Church

Details of 2 faces from the original 'Tiffany Studios' windows.

Details of 2 faces from Bovard Studio's new window titled 'Angels'. Notice the herringbone textured glass used for the angel's wings (left) and the drapery glass used in the angel's robe (right).

window drapery glass shimmers with all of the shadings of draped fabric in a robe or other draped garment. For the angel's wings, we selected a herringbone textured glass that is made in a similar fashion by pulling and manipulating the glass while in a semi-molten state.

We set about the task of selecting the glass for this project from the approximately 4,000 colors and textures that we have available. If we can't find the exact color or effect that we need, we will use the plating technique to increase our choices. Plating increases the choices exponentially, for example two pieces of glass plated together would give us 4,000 x 4,000 = 16 million possible color and texture choices. Of course, we do not have a lifetime to test all of these possibilities. Selecting the glass for any project is a highly intuitive process that is even more complex for a project such as this one.

We use a team approach that enables the leaded glass artists to collect input from other experienced glass artists on our staff. As the glass is selected and cut it is 'waxed up' (attached using a sticky wax) onto a glass easel that is placed in front of a natural light window facing the same direction as the completed window will face when it is installed. This is important so that we can examine the effects of the layered plates of glass in the same lighting conditions that the completed installed stained glass window will experience.

During this process our glass painters are sketching out full size drawings of the flesh (faces, hands and feet) areas of the new window and are planning how the plates are going to work in our Angels window.

Tiffany wanted to create stained glass windows that portray the brilliance and magic of the great glass of Europe's spectacular medieval cathedrals. Louis Tiffany felt that the windows being created by his generation of glass artists with their heavily painted stained glass had lost the magic of stained glass's glowing past glories. Tiffany wanted to create new stained glass windows that would be as magical and brilliant as past generations' best contributions.

Tiffany's philosophy was to limit glass painting to the flesh areas of a stained glass window. He created the balance and movement in his windows through the purity of the glass itself. Tiffany developed a variety of glasses to help him achieve his goal. They include opalescent glass, textured glass, plus other techniques such as plating and copper foiling to achieve all of the details and richness for his art images. The magic and brilliance of his treasured creations speak for themselves.

Our challenge here is to capture as much of that magic and brilliance as possible in this new creation. Our task has been made easier as the many Tiffany restorations we have completed over the years have revealed many of the master's secrets to us. But, there is one ingredient we are missing: the hands and eyes of the master himself.

Now our meticulous glass craftspeople take over and we painstakingly assemble the window. The assembly of plates and drapery glass requires large and uneven thicknesses of lead came. Our master craftspeople use the same fabricating techniques they have developed to restore the originals, often making the unique sizes and shapes of the lead came by hand.

After much work and concentration this window was complete and the day for installation finally arrived. The church congregation was thrilled. Examine these photos to judge for yourself just how close we came to capturing some of Louis Comfort Tiffany's magic in our new Angels window.

Bovard's finished and installed 'Angels' window.

A Small Brotherhood

AMID THE HILLS of north central Alabama, shrouded in early morning fog set ablaze by the afternoon sun, you will find the unassuming seat of the reign of silence. A profound spiritual silence, produced by the purity of monastic lives, enables a common civilian such as myself to feel God's presence.

Dedications abound with "God Incarnate" and "Christ the King", His name and form shapes this holy atmosphere in addition to the ceaseless devotion of a small brotherhood of traditional Benedictine Monks devoted to the ancient ways of the Roman Catholic Church.

Father Leonard, devoted priest, faithfully followed a steady course along the straight and narrow path of life-long dedication to his Church. Then soon after the implementation of Vatican II, he found himself at large in the wilderness outside of Mother Church. His life of single-minded devotion to God soon energized the forces of nature to reward Father Leonard's purity of heart. A parcel of property was secured and a small group of devoted like-minded souls united to raise Christ the King Abbey surrounded by the ancient forest in the hills of Alabama.

On my most recent trip to the Abbey, I was accompanied by my three youngest sons, Michael 15, Matthew 13, and 8 year old Johnny. As we wound our way up the serpentine driveway in our pickup truck, complete with camper and speedboat, these robust and dynamic boys quickly zeroed in on the Abbey as a spiritual beacon. Our motley crew became uncharacteristically tranquil as we approached the refuge. Cramped from long days of driving, my boys stumbled out of our cluttered truck inspired and awe-struck by the serene and holy atmosphere. We were warmly greeted by Father Abbot and the Monks

New installation of stained glass for Christ the King Abbey, Cullman, Alabama.

Christit the King Abbey

Interior view of Christ the King Abbey, note the circular window above the alter.

who reverently showed my sons the monastery church, which was built using very sketchy plans combined with much prayer and manual labor.

The Abbey is a repository of ancient knowledge and holy artifacts, which includes one of the most precious of all holy relics, a splinter from the cross upon which Christ was crucified. My sons, now completely taken up with the sacred ambience, were shown the historic personification of the saints as illustrated in the Gothic style stained glass windows that were created by our studio for the Abbey.

Soon enough my sons discovered Ginger, a stray dog adopted by the Abbey and while they all enjoyed a romp in the sun, the Monks and I discussed the design and plans for the monastery's final stained glass window, "Christ the King" (see this window on page 119, top left).

Nearing the end of our day, we were led down to the cool chambers of the guest dining room located under the sanctuary. Once there, we were treated to a vegetarian feast. As we quietly dined, we were enthralled by the echoes of the Monk's Gregorian chants of holy praise drifting down the corridors as they dined separately from us in ancient monastic tradition.

For the remainder of the trip, no matter how fine the restaurant, my sons would often remark, "Dad this food is good, but not as good as the food at the monastery!"

New installation of stained glass for Christ the King Abbey, Cullman, Alabama.

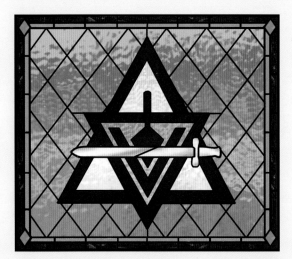

Masonic Symbols in Glass

MASONIC RETIREMENT CENTER, ARLINGTON, TEXAS

The long curving "Dallas style" driveway and extended horizontal lines of the Masonic home for aged Masons, called to mind of the significant history of this organization. Masonic Orders revolutionized feudal Europe with their spiritual and philosophical teachings which advanced the freeing of the serfs and led to the beginning of democratic government, culminating in a substantial contribution to the founding principles of the United States of America.

George Washington was the commander of his Masonic lodge and most of the signers of the Declaration of Independence were Freemasons. Our great nation was founded upon many principles of Freemasonry.

We were delighted to receive the contract to design and build the stained glass windows for the Masonic home's chapel. We worked closely with the Masons working out the computer aided designs for the renderings, communicating back and forth both graphically and verbally to get the designs and coloring of their symbolism exactly right for their chapel stained glass windows.

George Washington was the commander of his Masonic lodge and most of the signers of the Declaration of Independence were members of the Freemasons. For this reason alone it could be said that the Masonic philosophy contributed to the founding principles of the United States of America.

This series of new windows were designed for The Masonic Retirement Center Chapel in Arlington, Texas. The colors and attributes of this organization's distinctive symbolism has considerable significance and had to be exactly right for their chapel windows.

EASTERN VISIONS OF THE SOUL

5000 Years of Culture

THE MYSTERIOUS EAST with its more than 5,000 year old Vedic culture has much to offer the West. Many of their age-old herbal formulas have been proven to have dramatic effects on improving health without the side effects of our western pharmaceuticals. Eastern spiritual practices and philosophies are having an increasing impact on our own culture and world view. The recent revival of ancient meditation techniques is gaining popularity in the West. Significant bodies of scientific research are proving profound health benefits from these ancient practices and herbal formulas. That may help account for the practitioners' empirical reports of finding inner peace and fulfillment.

Hanuman has a powerful, muscular body and the superior intellect of a yogi. As the quintessential devotee he represents physical prowess, mental discipline and spiritual purity.

Bovard Studio has had the good fortunate to be awarded a number of commissions to create stained glass windows for this time-honored traditional culture. There is no better way to express the religious heritage and culture of ancient India, whose goal is enlightenment, than through the medium of light. As suriya, the sun moves across the eternal sky, each day new light is transformed by the stained glass window into art radiating through the inner space of the installations environment into the viewers eyes, mind, and soul.

Ganesha or Ganapati is the destroyer of all obstacles. He also represents education, knowledge, wisdom, literature, and the fine arts. This window was designed and built for a restaurant in Davenport, Iowa.

Lakshmi represents wealth, fortune, power, beauty, and abundance. She is enchantingly beautiful draped in a red sari, standing on a lotus blossom and holding lotus flowers in her hands. The white elephant, symbol of rain clouds showers her with water to bring life to parched land.

A Tiffany Restoration

RESTORING AN ORIGINAL TIFFANY WINDOW

The restoration of any historic window is a great responsibility for both the window's trustee and the contractor. The owner or trustee of the stained glass window must ensure that the restoration company has the training and experience to undertake all necessary work in a professional manner. References should be provided (and checked) and an extensive plan of action must be submitted by the contractor outlining the full extent of restoration, including adherence to historic conservation procedures. Comprehensive insurance must be engaged to safeguard against any perils that could occur to the window during removal, rebuilding and re-installation or at the very least the building's current insurance coverage needs to be extended for off premises work.

Right: An exquisite window by Louis C. Tiffany & Co. installed in St. Luke's United Methodist Church in Dubuque, Iowa, restored by Bovard Studio. Photo by Richard Gross.

When prestigious works by distinguished artists such as a L.C. Tiffany, J. LaFarge, F.L. Wright or others needs to be restored, it may be advisable to engage the services of a professional conservation consultant, specializing in stained glass restoration. It is advisable to locate a consultant that is a member of a licensed architectural firm. They will advise the trustee on the extent of work necessary and inform them on specific technical requirements to ensure that irreversible restoration methods are not undertaken. Historic restoration is definitely a job that is worth doing right and should be entrusted only to those who have proven to be trustworthy.

The first step in restoring any historic stained glass window is to document its current physical state and appearance. It is of the utmost importance to photograph the stained glass window in both transmitted and reflected light prior to removing it from its frame.

Take several photos of the window with transmitted light, (natural light passing through the stained glass) without flash and being careful that the interior lighting is extinguished. Since the exposure time will be longer (due to lower available light) it is advisable to mount the camera on a tripod when taking photographs from the interior side of the stained glass window.

Next make a record of the interior and exterior surfaces of the stained glass window in reflected light (lighted from the same side as the camera). The sun's light will usually suffice for the exterior photos but a supplemental flash may be needed for the interior surface photographs. Separate photos should be taken for each stained glass panel (section) of the window, plus detailed photos of specific areas with extensive damage such as cracked glass, missing areas of glass, badly damaged paint, etc. Additional photographic documentation may be made back at the studio if required.

Prepare the windows for removal by securing loose and/or broken pieces of glass with conservators tape. It is always advisable to secure the entire width and length of the panel with tape, especially if the window's structure is weak and fragile. It is important to check any painted areas for

The first step in restoring any historic stained glass window is to photograph its current physical state in both transmitted and reflected light prior to removing it from its frame. Photo by Richard Gross.

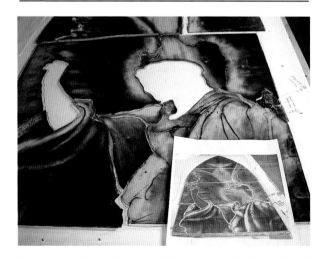

Every window is photographed in detail prior to removal, then another set of photos is taken in the restoration studio before disassembly. A color printout is made to help us keep meticulous project notes as the pieces are removed.

Above: Mickey Bar and Paul Conley of Bovard Studio are shown here carrying a section of Tiffany's "Job" window. Note the conservators tape used to enhance stability during shipping.

stability prior to placing conservators tape on these surfaces. If the glass paint is unstable or the stability of the paint is in doubt, the painted side of the stained glass must not be taped. Once the panels have been secured, they are carefully removed from the window frame and placed into wooden packing crates with foam rubber sheeting to separate and protect the fragile panels during transport. We pickup and deliver the panels in our own trucks.

Once back at the shop, the extracted stained glass windows are prepared for restoration. The first panel is placed onto the glazing bench where more notes are taken and more photographs made (if necessary). Then a rubbing is made for each section of the window by placing vellum paper over the window and rubbing colored oil pastels (or artists charcoal) over the lead lines to create a full size pattern of the lead matrix. This pattern will be used later for reassembly. If the section contains plating, as the Tiffany window in the illustration does, a separate rubbing is made for each layer of plate. These additional plate rubbings are done on top of the first rubbing using a different colored pastel for each successive layer of plating (a rubbing is made after each plate layer is removed). This will show the

These valuable windows are painstakingly disassembled. The leads are clipped and the cement is removed until the glass piece is loose. Prying or pushing the delicate glass to remove it is risky and these suction cup grippers come in very handy.

Each piece of glass is numbered and photographed immediately after it is detached from the window. We use these photos to help us do any necessary repairs, keep track of the colors and help to reposition the glass pieces after they are cleaned.

fabricator how each plate is "registered" on the window during reassembly. Notes are taken of the size, profile and description of each lead came or copper foil area within the stained glass window and this is recorded directly on the rubbing. Then two copies of each rubbing are made one for reference and one as a working copy.

The restoration specialist must be sure that sufficient records have been made to ensure an exact reconstruction can be achieved. Only then are the stained glass panels carefully disassembled. The lead came is cut away and one glass piece at a time is removed and placed in it's correct location on the working copy of the rubbing. During disassembly it is important to keep a sample of each different lead came size and profile or a section of the copperfoil assembly for reference and documentation.

When the entire panel has been disassembled it must be cleaned and inspected. Each piece of non-painted glass is cleaned with Triton X-100, a professional quality, non-ionic detergent (made by City Chemical Company of NY) or an equivalent pH neutral glass cleaner mixed with distilled water. Prior to cleaning, painted areas of the window must be tested to determine that the paint is stable. If it is, these areas should be gently cleaned with a soft cotton cloth and distilled water. Unstable painted areas need be stabilized. The basic treatment is to coat the painted surface with a restoration grade clear fixative to bond the remaining paint to the glass. However, it is intensely important that the fixative used be chemically compatible with the underlying paint to

A close-up side view of a Tiffany window showing the use of molded glass for the flower. Note how the flower petals protrude from the surface of the window.

Above & Right: Detail photograph of the same figure shown before and after cleaning the dirt out from between the glass plates. The difference is dramatic especially in the angel's hair and wings.

ensure no further damage is induced. For this reason it is necessary to consult an expert restoration specialist to determine the appropriate consolidation method for the particular problem encountered. Areas where the paint is badly faded, has been washed away, or otherwise lost, should be restored by first treating the existing paint with the clear fixative. Then the missing details are painted onto a new piece of 1/16" (1.5 mm) or thinner clear glass that is plated over the original painted stained glass. This ensures the historic work remains unaltered and undisturbed and makes the restoration fully reversible in the future.

Cracked and broken pieces of stained glass are repaired by edge gluing with clear Hxtel™ epoxy (a commercial brand product), clear silicone, or by copper foiling and soldering the pieces together. The specific repair method will be decided based upon what is best for the historic preservation of the particular stained glass window.

Left: Ascension of Christ by Tiffany Studios at St. Luke's United Methodist Church, Dubuque, Iowa, restored by Bovard Studio. Photo by Richard Gross.

Below: Interior of St. Luke United Methodist Church showing the restored "Job" window in the balcony among the other exquisite Tiffany Windows all restored by Bovard Studio. Photo by Richard Gross.

Tiffany Restoration

Missing pieces of art glass can sometimes be closely matched from the more than 4,000 colors, densities and textures that are manufactured and available today. If a close match cannot be found from available glass, you can plate two layers of stained glass together to produce a third color and texture. If necessary several plates can be combined to give the stained glass restoration artist countless possibilities. In some cases where a glass making formula is known, a glass manufacturer may be willing to custom create a particular stained glass sheet to match a destroyed original piece. This is an expensive alternative but if the missing glass is dominant in the design or if the window is an exceptional work, this may be the best solution.

The various sizes and profiles of lead came also need to be closely matched. Many of the came profiles are available as standard stock items manufactured from existing dies, however other more specialized shapes may need to be specially ordered from custom or rarely used dies and depending on the importance of the window, may be a necessary step. Other cames are hand made for a perfect match.

Once all the glass has been cleaned, broken pieces repaired, missing pieces replaced, painted pieces replicated, and all other materials are obtained, the stained glass window is ready to be reassembled. The pieces will be placed on the working copy of the rubbing, precisely as the window was originally created. The fabrication will be carried out by skilled craftsmen in essentially the same tried and true method as the window was fabricated decades before.

Above: The top section of the 'Annunciation' window by Louis Tiffany and Company during disassembly for restoration. This window is being restored from fire damage at St. John's Episcopal Church, Quincy, Illinois.

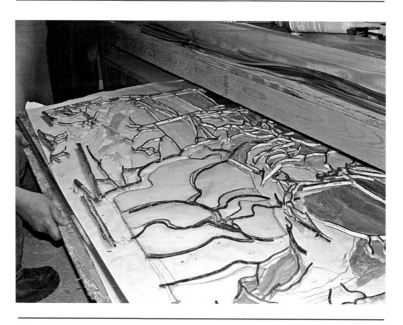

The bottom panel of the 'Annunciation' window. The lead came profiles are recorded and retained for documentation purposes to assist in reassembly.

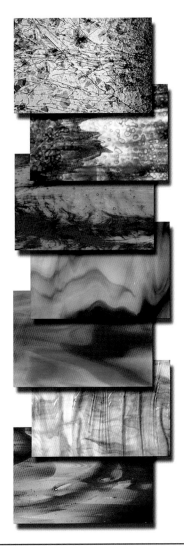

The Tiffany window we are restoring here has complex plated sections that will require the fabricator to devise an assembly of lead cames to create a shape otherwise not available. They will solder several strips and/or layers of came together to create a shape based on the sample saved during disassembly. We have found that a modern improvement can be made to the original structure of plated sections by applying a silicone seal around the edges of the stacked plates of glass. This will prevent dirt and water from collecting between the plates, which cannot be cleaned without disassembling the window. Contamination of plated sections is a major problem encountered in historic windows that include extensive plating.

Any structural deficiencies in the original windows should be addressed to prevent the premature failure of the window in the future. One major structural remedy is to use lead came that has sufficient tensile strength. It is crucial to use a lead came manufactured by the extrusion process using a lead alloy that contains antimony, silver, copper, or tin. The original stained glass window was probably fabricated using pure milled lead (without alloy additives) which is comparatively soft and malleable (lead alloy came is a recent development). This improvement alone will greatly increase the expected longevity of the stained glass restoration. Another common structural deficiency is the use of a single layer of relatively thin glass, usually 1/8" (3 mm), in the borders. This fragile border is required to support the heavy weight of the central glass section and is particularly troublesome in windows with multiple plates of glass which add considerable weight. Unfortunately, this situation often results in the folding and sometimes total collapse of the border, especially at the base and lower sides of the window. A simple, reversible, non-invasive

Above: We can can usually closely match the missing pieces from the more than 4000 art glass selections manufactured and available today.

Right: One of the last windows made by Tiffany Studios in 1931, titled David Sets Singers Before The Lord. Installed in St. Luke's United Methodist Church, restored by Bovard Studio. *Photo by Richard Gross.*

Tiffany Restoration

remedy for this deficiency is to apply a second plate of clear glass to the border areas on the exterior side of the window, thereby doubling the strength of the borders.

When fabrication is complete, the window must be cemented with a glazing cement specifically formulated for leaded windows. The cementing process packs the space between the flanges of the lead came and the stained glass with a sealant to stiffen and strengthen the window as well as weatherproof it. Most cement compounds have a black dye component to enhance the surface the new "silvery colored" lead with a dark, richly colored patina to give it a more mature appearance.

During a restoration such as this Tiffany window, we take special notice of areas with the most structural damage. These areas of distress may be due to an insufficient supporting structure or to weaknesses within the windows design.

Above: Detail of The Baptism of Christ window by Tiffany Studios 1916, restored by Bovard Studio. Photo by Richard Gross.

Right: Louis Tiffany's masterpiece, The Good Shepherd, was exhibited in the 1893 at the World Columbian Exhibition and contains some of the finest glass produced by his company. This window was purchased in 1896 by Judge D. N. Cooley's family and was installed as a memorial to him and his wife at St. Luke's Church. Bovard Studio was selected to restore this historic Tiffany in 2002.

Tiffany Restoration

Above: The fabrication will be carried out by skilled craftsmen in essentially the same tried and true method as it was decades before. This plated window was damaged in a fire and is a restoration for First Evangelical Lutheran Church, Altoona, PA.

Detail from Christ Blessing The Children by Tiffany Studios 1916, restored by Bovard Studio for St. Luke's United Methodist Church, Dubuque, Iowa. Photo by Richard Gross.

Whatever the reason it is our responsibility to correct the problem in the least intrusive way. Obviously these areas require additional structural engineering and one of the most effective solutions is to attach brass rebar directly to the lead in the structurally deficient areas of the window. This rebar is a flat brass rod, 1/16" (1.5 mm) thick and anywhere from 1/4" to 1" (6.3 to 25.4 mm) wide. It is soldered directly to the lead came, perpendicular (90°) to the face, on the exterior side of the window. Preferably these rebars should be kept as straight as possible but they may be bent to follow along the length of a gently curving lead line. This technique structurally reinforces the stained glass window with minimum aesthetic impact.

While the stained glass window is "in the shop" undergoing restoration, it's an opportune time to take up the necessary repairs and restoration to the window's frame. In some extreme cases the frame may need to be totally replaced, at the very least it should be cleaned, sealed and refinished. If the window restoration company does not provide these services, a qualified carpenter should be called to make an assessment of the frame's integrity and complete the repairs.

The culmination of any restoration is the time of reinstallation, when the restored window is returned to its rightful home. A scrupulously restored window, with structural weaknesses remedied and installed with a properly vented protective covering (see pages 60-65), can be expected to last significantly longer than the original stained glass window, before it will require another restoration.

It is a very gratifying experience to return a Tiffany or other historic stained glass window to its original appearance and condition. It is rewarding to witness the dramatic contrast between the dirty, deteriorated, misshapen window of the past to the richness of color and structural integrity of the restored installation. It is a thrill to return the many lost details of a window, details that seemed to be hidden in the past and are now mysteriously resurrected into the living present.

Below: The completed and installed restoration of the Tiffany "Job" window at St. Luke's Church. Photo by Richard Gross.

Above: Paul Conley (left) and Mike Swope (right) install one section of the restored "Job" window.

The Stained Glass Design Gallery

THE DESIGNS on the following 52 pages presents a cross section of work taken from Bovard Studio's portfolio. From simple to complex, abstract to representational, traditional to modern and from small intimate stained glass windows to windows as big as the side of a building. The techniques used to fabricate these windows varies from lead came and copper foil to epoxy resin (for faceted glass). Some designs have little or no glass painting while others have every piece of glass in the window painted. Some windows use etching, others have silver staining, plating, traditional glass staining colors, transparent and opaque enamels, stenciling, silk screening and/or medallions. The vast majority of the window designs have a combination of several of these treatments.

On these pages you will find a wide variety of what is possible in ecclesiastic art glass today. It is our hope that you will find inspiration from a few of them, and it will be a step in your continued exploration of the art and the craft of stained glass.

Reference BB100

Reference BB101

Reference BB102

Reference BB103

Reference BB104

Reference BB105

Reference BB106

Reference BB107

Reference BB108

Reference BB109

Reference BB110

Reference BB111

Reference BB112

Reference BB113

Reference BB114

Reference BB115

Reference BB116

Reference BB117

Reference BB118

Reference BB119

Reference BB130

Reference BB131

Reference BB132

Reference BB134

Reference BB136

Reference BB137

Reference BB133

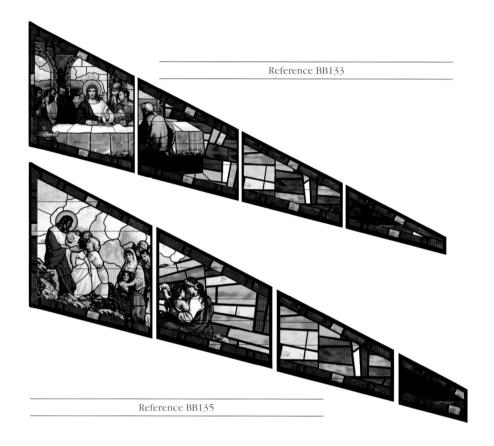

Reference BB135

Reference BB137

Reference BB138

Reference BB139

Reference BB140

Reference BB141

Reference BB142

Reference BB143

Reference BB144

Reference BB145

Reference BB146

Reference BB147

Reference BB148

Reference BB149

The Design Gallery

Reference BB153

Reference BB154

Reference BB155

Reference BB150

Reference BB151

Reference BB152

Reference BB156

Reference BB157

Reference BB158

Reference BB159

Reference BB160

Reference BB161

Reference BB162

Reference BB163

Reference BB164

Reference BB165

Reference BB166

Reference BB167

Reference BB168

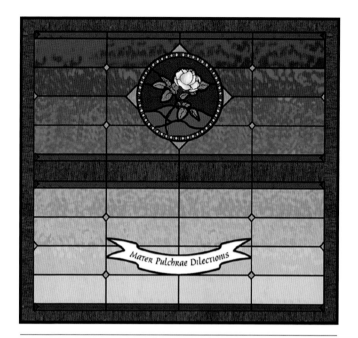

Reference BB169

Reference BB170

Reference BB171

Reference BB172

Reference BB173

Reference BB174

Reference BB175

Reference BB176

Reference BB177

Reference BB178

Reference BB179

Reference BB180

Reference BB181

Reference BB183

Reference BB182

Reference BB184

Reference BB185

Reference BB186

Reference BB187

Reference BB189

Reference BB188

Reference BB191

Reference BB190

Reference BB192

Reference BB193

Reference BB194

Reference BB195

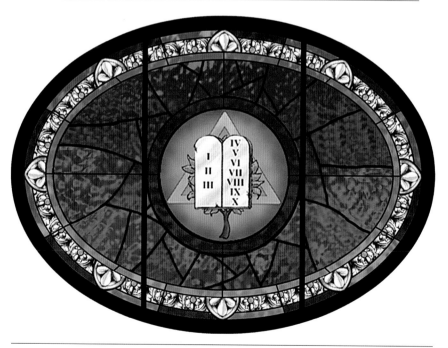

Reference BB196

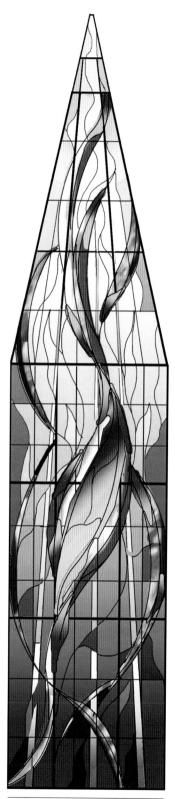

Reference BB197

Creation - Reference BB198

Reference BB199

Noah's Ark - Reference BB200

Reference BB201

Birth of Christ - Reference BB202

Baptism of Christ - Reference BB203

Crucifixion - Reference BB204

Resurrection - Reference BB205

Reference BB206

Reference BB207

IN MEMORY OF
IVAN & CATHERINE SNOWDEN

IN MEMORY OF
EDWARD & JOHANNA CONNELL

Reference BB208

Reference BB209

Reference BB210

Reference BB211

Reference BB212

Reference BB213

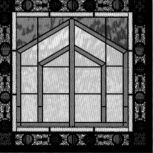

Reference BB214

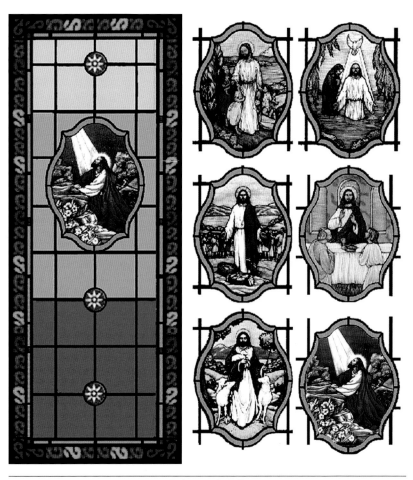

Reference BB215

Reference BB216

Reference BB217

Reference BB218

Reference BB219

Reference BB220

Reference BB221

Reference BB222

Reference BB223

Reference BB224

Reference BB225

Reference BB226

Reference BB227

Reference BB228

Reference BB229

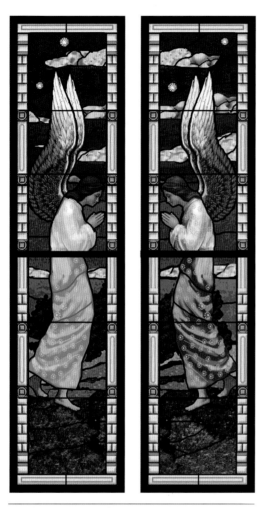

Reference BB230

Reference BB231

Reference BB232

Reference BB233

Reference BB234

Reference BB235

Reference BB236

Reference BB237

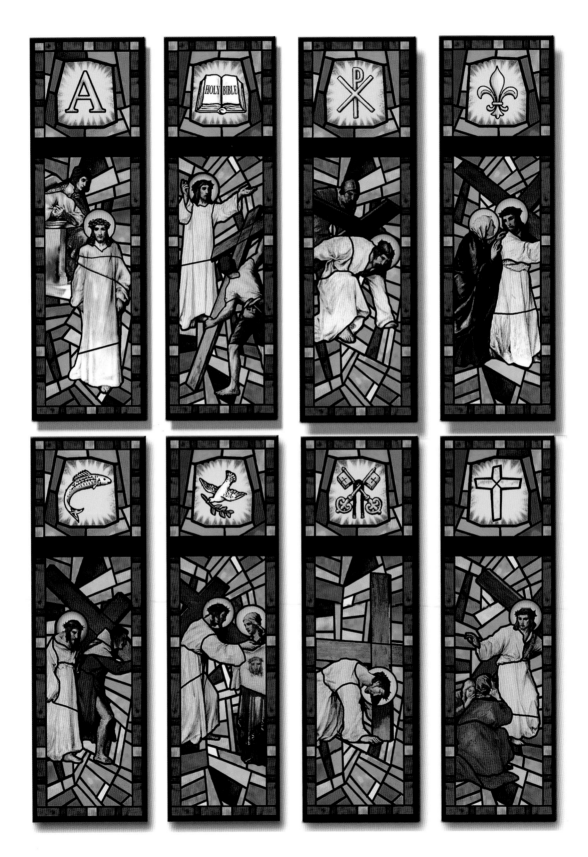

THE 14 STATIONS OF THE CROSS • Reference B238

The Faceted Glass Design Gallery

DALLE DE VERRE (French for "tiles of glass") is commonly referred to as faceted glass. It is an epoxy-resin cast glass window that uses dalles (slabs) of glass that are made by pouring molten glass into an 8" x 12" x 1" deep mold (20 x 30 x 2.5 cm). These dalles are available in a wide range of colors in shades from light to dark. The dalles cut and shaped using a steel tool to create the edge facets (hence the name) designed to catch and refract the light (notice these facets in the window below).

The surface of the epoxy-resin is usually finish coated with a natural sand aggregate in colors such as white, grey and most commonly black. The epoxy-resin will adhere to almost any porous texture, so other materials could be used if desired.

For more information on faceted glass and the manufacturing process see Chapter 21 on page 80.

Reference BB239

Reference BB240

Reference BB242

Reference BB241

Reference BB243

Reference BB244

Reference BB245

Reference BB246

Reference BB247

Reference BB2048

Reference BB249

Reference BB251

Reference BB250

Reference BB252

Reference BB253

Reference BB254

Reference BB255

Reference BB256

Reference BB257

Reference BB259

Reference BB258

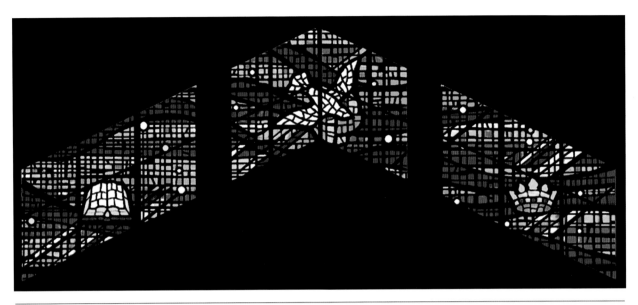

Reference BB260

Reference BB261

Reference BB262

Reference BB263

Reference BB264

The Rose Window Design Gallery

A ROSE WINDOW is generally defined as a circular stained glass window with mullions and traceries that radiate from the centre. It is believed that the name 'Rose Window' alludes to the Virgin Mary who is often referred to as the Mystical Rose in religious literature.

The origin of a large round window in church architecture can be traced back to round opening in the top of the dome of the Pantheon in Rome, Italy. This opening in the ceiling is called a Roman oculus (Latin for eye) that was eventually transformed during the Romanesque period to become a large round window framed into a wall.

ROSE WINDOW GALLERY

Reference BB265

Reference BB266

Reference BB267

Reference BB268

Reference BB269

Reference BB270

Reference BB271

Reference BB272

Reference BB273

Chapter 30 – The Rose Window Design Gallery

Reference BB274

Reference BB275

Reference BB276

Reference BB277

Reference BB278

Reference BB279

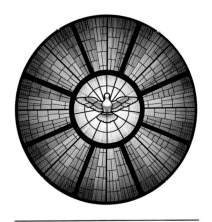

Reference BB280

Reference BB281

Reference BB282

Reference BB283

Reference BB284

Reference BB285

Reference BB286

Reference BB287

Reference BB288

Reference BB289

Reference BB290

Reference BB291

Reference BB292

Reference BB293

Reference BB294

Reference BB295

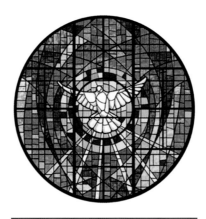

Reference BB296

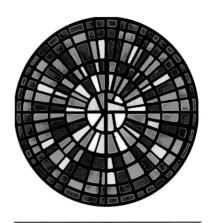

Reference BB297

Reference BB298

Reference BB299

Reference BB300

Reference BB301

Reference BB302

Reference BB303

Reference BB304

Reference BB305

Reference BB306

Reference BB307

Reference BB308

Reference BB309

Reference BB310

Reference BB311

Reference BB312

Reference BB313

Reference BB314

Reference BB315

Reference BB316

Reference BB317

Reference BB318

Reference BB319

Reference BB320

Reference BB321

Reference BB322

Reference BB323

Reference BB324

Reference BB325

Reference BB326

Reference BB327

Reference BB328

Reference BB329

Reference BB330

Reference BB331

Reference BB332

Reference BB333

Reference BB334

Reference BB335

Reference BB336

Author's Journal

SINCE 1971 THE WORK of Ron Bovard has been exhibited at galleries and museums around the world, including the Carnegie Museum of Art. Bovard has had more than twenty-five one-man exhibits. Four of these were at prestigious New York City galleries and three at Vienna, Austria galleries, including his 1984 one-man exhibit at Galerie Kunst Depot during the world famous Vienna Festival. Enthusiastic critiques and reviews of Mr. Bovard's art have been carried in many newspapers and magazines, including The Pittsburgh Press, The New Yorker, and New York's Art Speak. Ron Bovard's artwork has been written about in books published in two languages, distributed in North America and Europe. In addition he has participated in many radio interviews and has been featured in several television programs, including three programs for regional PBS network affiliates.

Some excerpts from what the Critics said about Ron Bovard's Art:

• GREAT ART… "A savvy hayseed…Reminiscent of Grandma Moses…A kissing cousin of that other savvy hayseed Red Grooms" -Art Speak, New York

• ENVIRONMENTAL… "One continuous landscape travels around the four walls of West Broadway" - The New Yorker; "Painting works spatially, communicating a sense of expansion" - Altoona Mirror

• BEAUTY… "…enjoyed for color and design qualities" - Pittsburgh Press; "Rich innocent imagery" - Fairfield Ledger; "His art is pervaded by a peace that is transcendental in nature." - Altoona Mirror

• CONTENT… "This image has the force to counteract our post-industrial fate" - Art Speak, New York; "Simple, charming and innocent" - Ottumwa Courier; "Full of mystery and symbolism" - Pittsburgh Press

• SPIRITUALLY UPLIFTING… "Cosmic" - Pittsburgh Post Gazette; "Represents nature's underlying unmanifest field of being" - Altoona Mirror

SELECTED ONE MAN SHOWS:

• Nov 1987 - Merrill Gallery, Kansas City, MO, USA

• July 1984 - Galerie Flora, Vienna, Austria

• May 1984 - Galerie Kunst Depo, Vienna, Austria

• Sep 1983 - Westbroadway Gallery, New York, NY USA

• Apr 1983 - Lynn Kottler Gallery, New York, NY USA

• Jan 1982 - Alternate Space Gallery, New York, NY USA

• Oct 1980 - Undercroft Gallery, Pittsburgh, PA USA

AUTHOR'S SHOW JOURNAL

Contact Information

CONTACT (vertical sidebar text) **INFORMATION**

CONTACT BOVARD STUDIO

Bovard Studio Inc

2281 Highway 34 East,

Fairfield, IA 52556 USA

Phone: (641) 472-2824

Fax:　　(641) 472-0974

E-mail: info@bovardstudio.com

WEB SITE ADDRESSES

WINDOWS FOR THE SOUL - WEBSITE
www.windowsforthesoul.com

BOVARD STUDIO - WEBSITE
www.bovardstudio.com

WARDELL PUBLICATIONS - WEBSITE
www.wardellpublications.com

BIBLIOGRAPHY

Note: For more details on sources and resources contained in this book please log onto the book's official web site at: www.windowsforthesoul.com

• Nolte, Carl, Chronicle Staff Writer, "Landmark Church Rebuilt After Fire. Dedication Today to Celebrate New St. Peter's" San Francisco Chronicle, June 30, 2000.

• Calvet, Jill, "Extreme: Celebrating Superlatives: The Oldest Stained Glass Windows," Ambassador Magazine, Boston and St. Louis: Ambassador Inflight Marketing, January, 1999.

• Elskus, Albinas. The Art of Painting on Glass: Techniques and Designs for Stained Glass. New York: Charles Scribner's Sons, 1980.

• Art Business News, Stamford, CT: Myers Publishing Co., Inc. (general source)

• Glass: History, Manufacture and Its Universal Applications. Pittsburgh, Pennsylvania: Pittsburgh Plate Glass Company, 1923.

• Inspired Partnerships, Inc., Chicago, IL, "Protective Glazing Study June 1996" for the National Center for Technology and Training, Nachitoches, Louisiana. Available on the NCPTT website: http://www.ncptt.nps.gov

• Sloan, Julie L., "PSG Restoration Report: Protective Glazing." Stained Glass Restoration & Preservation. Published quarterly by Professional Stained Glass magazine –Volume 1, No. 1 – Spring 1990. Brewster, New York: The Edge Publishing Group, Inc.

• Stained Glass Quarterly of the Stained Glass Association of America. Kansas City, Missouri: The Stained Glass Association of America. (general source)

• SGAA Reference & Technical Manual: A Comprehensive Guide To Stained Glass. Kansas City, Missouri: The Staincd Glass Association of America, 1992

• Standards and Guidelines for the Preservation of Historic Stained Glass. Kansas City, Missouri: The Stained Glass Association of America, revised November 1998

• Our National Historic Landmark, The Plum Street Temple, Must Be Preserved," by Rabbi Alan D. Fuchs and Joseph S. Stern, Jr.

Wardell
PUBLICATIONS INC
Instruction, Inspiration and Innovation for the Art Glass Communnity

  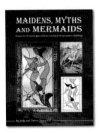  

    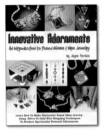 

  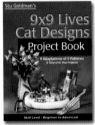   

    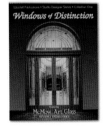 

e-mail: info@wardellpublications.com website: www.wardellpublications.com